IMMIGRATION, POLICY AND THE PEOPLE OF LATIN AMERICA

Taking on historical events in Latin America as its starting point, this book examines the migration of its inhabitants to the United States with case studies from seven nations: Colombia, Cuba, Haiti, Honduras, Guatemala, Mexico, and Venezuela.

Combining the disciplines of history and law, the authors explore the economic and historical challenges present in each nation that force "out" migration, including corruption, historical exploitation, racism, unequal/unfair trade arrangements, and the oftentimes unilateral, exploitative operations of multinational corporations. Readers will learn about the contemporary socio/political and economic realities of the seven sending nations and understand the complexity of immigration laws (as passed by the Congress), executive actions taken by individual presidents in the United States, and some state initiatives. They will hear the voices of immigrants themselves, as well as those who have stayed behind or been deported from the United States back to their home nations.

This book will be of interest to students of Latin American history, as well as US history and politics.

Bryce W. Ashby is an attorney with Donati Law, PLLC, where he represents workers in their employment law claims. He is a graduate of the University of Memphis Cecil C. Humphreys School of Law and Rhodes College and was a Peace Corps Volunteer in Honduras from 2000 to 2002.

Michael J. LaRosa is an associate professor of history at Rhodes College. He focuses on contemporary Colombian history and has published work in collaboration with Germán R. Mejía, Frank O. Mora, and others.

Latin American Tópicos

Edited by Michael LaRosa, Rhodes College

Telenovelas in Pan-Latino Context
June Carolyn Erlick

The Youngest Citizens
Amy Risley

Latin American Soldiers
Armed Forces in the Region's History
John R. Bawden

Natural Disasters in Latin America and the Caribbean
Coping with Calamity
June Carolyn Erlick

Public Health and Beyond in Latin America and the Caribbean
Reflections from the Field
Sherri L. Porcelain

Essays on 20th Century Latin American Art
Francine Birbragher-Rozencwaig

Latin American Economic History
An Introduction to Daily Life, Debt, and Development
Molly C. Ball

Immigration, Policy and the People of Latin America
Seven Sending Nations
Bryce W. Ashby and Michael J. LaRosa

For more information about this series, please visit:
www.routledge.com/Latin-American-Tpicos/book-series/LAT

"*Immigration, Policy and the People of Latin America: Seven Sending Nations* is a testament to Bryce W. Ashby and Michael J. LaRosa's unwavering dedication to scholarship and advocacy. With heartfelt insights and meticulous research, they illuminate the complexities of immigration from Latin America to the United States. As the former Executive Director of Latino Memphis, Inc., I commend their efforts in amplifying marginalized voices and challenging conventional narratives. This book is not just timely—it's essential reading for anyone seeking a deeper understanding of immigration issues."

José Velázquez, *Former Executive Director, Latino Memphis, Inc.*

"This book expertly captures the complex 'push' factors that drive immigration in much of the Americas, and brilliantly places them in their unique historical and political context by using a comparative, country-by-country approach. To contextualize these forces further, Ashby and LaRosa have focused—refreshingly—on the lives and journeys of individual immigrants. Lifting up this human dimension is essential for a full comprehension of the phenomena of migration and opens our hearts to the impacts these forces have on individuals, families, and communities."

David Lubell, *Founder and Director Emeritus—*
Welcoming America; Atlanta, Georgia

IMMIGRATION, POLICY AND THE PEOPLE OF LATIN AMERICA

Seven Sending Nations

Bryce W. Ashby and Michael J. LaRosa

Routledge
Taylor & Francis Group
NEW YORK AND LONDON

Designed cover image: Nicario Jiménez Q. Detail from *La Pesadilla*, 1998 (mixed media)

First published 2025
by Routledge
605 Third Avenue, New York, NY 10158

and by Routledge
4 Park Square, Milton Park, Abingdon, Oxon, OX14 4RN

Routledge is an imprint of the Taylor & Francis Group, an informa business

ISBN: 978-1-032-41338-9 (hbk)
ISBN: 978-1-032-40831-6 (pbk)
ISBN: 978-1-003-35760-5 (ebk)

DOI: 10.4324/9781003357605

Typeset in Sabon
by SPi Technologies India Pvt Ltd (Straive)

To all the immigrants who generously shared their stories with us

CONTENTS

MAPS

ACKNOWLEDGMENTS

A project of this scope requires support from many individuals. First, we'd like to acknowledge the anonymous reviewers who provided helpful suggestions as the proposal took shape. At Routledge in New York, we counted on the excellent editorial advice and support of Kimberley Smith and Allison Sambucini.

In Memphis, at Rhodes College, we were supported by Bonnie Burgette, Laura Jacobsen, and Tait Keller. Funding was provided through the Office of Fellowships and Undergraduate Research, directed by D. Brian Larkins. Provost Timothy Huebner assisted with additional funding at Rhodes College.

At the University of Memphis Law Library, Steven Richardson supported us with helpful legal advice.

All our interviewees were extremely generous with their time and shared very personal details of their travels to the United States. We wish we could have named them—many of them requested anonymity, and we decided to change the names of all interviewees.

Mr. Cody Stockton helped from Brooklyn, New York, as did Prof. Paul J. Angelo from Washington. Drew Hendrickson supported the project from Boston as did June C. Erlick from Cambridge, Massachusetts.

Alan Belitsky edited portions of this book from Tucson, and Nicario Jiménez offered advice from Naples, Florida. Judge Tanner Neidhardt helped from Austin, Texas, as did Prof. Steve Stein from Miami. Prof. Lina Del Castillo helped from Austin.

Lucy Fornetti and Cameron Bobbit, students at Rhodes College, helped with research and other details. Special thanks to Rhodes student Gwen Williams, who helped with research, editing, and all of the other details involved in producing a book. She also drew up the index—all during senior year of college!

INTRODUCTION

The United States is a nation of immigrants; we never imagined the way with which immigration would be used as a political tool—as per the Trump campaign and presidency. Never have Americans been more fully uninformed on the issue of immigration to the United States. The disinformation campaign is clear, compelling, and functional—i.e., it's profitable to those who sustain it. This includes politicians, members of the mainstream media, and educators who refuse to "educate" on the topic of immigration.

Both authors of this book have had the good fortune to live outside of the United States for extended periods of time. Bryce Ashby served in the United States Peace Corps upon graduation from college in 2000 and spent 27 months in Honduras. Michael LaRosa has lived in Colombia as a Fulbright scholar and professor for a total of about six years. Stepping outside our home nation, we've been able to understand more clearly what drives people to make the decision to change nations. Oftentimes, as is certainly the case of the nations we know best (and the other five nations we report on in this book), people make decisions that literally have life or death consequences.

We do not have a political agenda—we're not politicians. Mr. Ashby is an attorney and has been active in the local Hispanic outreach organization called "Latino Memphis, Inc.," and Michael LaRosa is a teacher and writer. Both authors are concerned that the immigration debate has been captured by political pundits and individuals who have a "scare" agenda, i.e., the use of immigration as a mechanism to frighten and manipulate people. This tactic has been at play since the middle of the 19th century when the "Know Nothing" party formed with the express purpose of frightening people in the United States into adopting an

DOI: 10.4324/9781003357605-1

anti-immigrant (mostly anti-Catholic, anti-German, and later anti-Irish) stance. The party faded away by 1860 but set a tone of anti-immigration in the United States that we haven't quite excoriated from society.

Our sole purpose in publishing this book at this time is to help educate the next generation and to explain the multiple interconnected factors that lead to immigration—factors that have contributed remarkably to America's greatness as a wealthy, powerful nation and a society that welcomes and encourages immigration. Nations that shut out immigrants tend to—in recent times—create stagnant economies. Italy and Japan come to mind. They've had negative economic growth rates for the past generation, and the formula of aging populations combined with harsh anti-immigration policies tends to supress economic growth. Simply put, as people grow older, they can't or don't work as hard, and they tend to be less productive in terms of physical labor.

As the US population ages, economic growth will be tied to immigrant labor and immigration in general. We can't build a wall to keep out immigrants; to do so is to commit economic and cultural suicide. The next generation of politicians will have to strike a balance between helping immigrants arrive here and assimilate versus the current trend in society that has focused on the fear factor. Always, in history, immigration sentiment moves as a pendulum, and right now, as we write in mid-2023, the scare tactics seem to be winning out.

In 2015, we watched a candidate for the presidency descend a golden escalator in New York City and launch his campaign by describing Mexican immigrants as "rapists and murderers." The battle effectively was engaged at that moment. From there, candidate Trump became president-elect Trump, and on January 20, 2017 via his "American Carnage" speech, Mr. Trump was inaugurated president. Within the first seven days of his administration, on January 27, 2017, the president signed an executive order that barred people from seven predominantly Muslim nations from traveling to the United States—the so-called "Muslim Ban."

This set the tone for the Trump Administration's policies toward immigration, immigrants, and those who were not quite American or capable of becoming American, in the eyes of the administration—i.e., Muslims, Mexicans, asylum seekers, people from the global south, and those from "Shit-hole" countries, President Trump's infamous term for people from Haiti and El Salvador (and several African nations) made in early January 2018 in the White House.

This book is designed to help students contextualize the most recent immigration dustups, but, more importantly, to place the immigration debate or non-debate in America in a global, historic context. Thus the historic approach, but readers will more thoroughly understand the recent histories of seven nations in Latin America, while comparing those histories to the broad arc of US immigration policy over the past one hundred years—going back to about 1924 when the first comprehensive immigration bill was passed by Congress.

The literature on immigration is rich and diverse. In 1890, a Danish journalist and social reformer Jacob Riis published *How the Other Half Lives*. This work of social history/photo journalism employed stark, clear black-and-white images to narrate a story of poverty, sadness, and human deprivation at a time of great economic prosperity and expansion in much of the United States. The focus of Riis's photo-journalistic gaze was recently arriving Italians and Jews who had migrated to New York from Russia, Poland, and other places in Europe that were inhospitable to practitioners of the Jewish faith.

Journalists Helen Thorp, Stephanie Elizondo Griest, Jorge Ramos, Sam Quinones, and Sonia Nazario have all published important works on immigration in the United States. Ediberto Román, a law professor and activist, published *Those Damned Immigrants: America's Hysteria over Undocumented Immigrants*. That book formed part of a series on immigration published by New York University Press and led to conversations that merged legal, political, and social concerns focused on immigration. The author "sensed," in his 2013 book, that something had changed regarding America's acceptance of immigrants: that something could have been the economic collapse of 2008–2009, or the election of the first African American president in 2008. The nation, but particularly the states of Alabama and Arizona, reacted with punitive legislation and sought out a historic scapegoat to the prevalent economic and social anxieties. This "story" plays out consistently in the aftermath of economic crisis, going back to at least the mid-19th century.

Writers, too, have addressed the immigration theme. Viet Than Nguyen has written about Vietnamese immigrants/refugees in the United States, and the Colombian-American lawyer/writer Sergio de la Pava has addressed this topic, focusing on Colombian immigrants in New York and New Jersey. Literature professor Oscar Cásares has published on immigrants to Texas (he wrote a compelling collection of short stories titled *Brownsville*), and, more recently, the Mexican writer Valeria Luiselli published a remarkably innovative novel that weaves into the narrative nonfiction elements titled *Lost Children Archives*. The book resonated with readers, critics, and the literary establishment given that it was released about a year and a half after the Trump Administration imposed its notorious "family separation" policy on families arriving at the US border. That policy was rescinded about a year after implementation, but the damage was—and has been—lasting, profound, and pervasive. Cormac McCarthy, who died in Santa Fe, New Mexico, as we prepared this book, understood the border between the United States and Mexico as ephemeral, metaphorical. In *All the Pretty Horses* (1991), he described the United States using a Mexican perspective: "Some had friends or relatives who had been there but to most the country to the north was little more than a rumor."

Immigration policy and implementation has had wide-reaching implications in US society and history. Recently, as mentioned above, the Trump Administration adopted (within the first six months of taking office) a "zero tolerance" policy whereby folks arriving to the United States without proper documentation were arrested—on misdemeanor charges (for first-time offenders) at the time; their underage children were taken away from them in a move that shocked most Americans and sent alarming signals to the international community. The Trump Administration is forever connected to this policy, and Mr. Trump, as of this writing, is seeking a second presidential term in 2024. He lost the 2020 presidential race in the middle of a global pandemic. During the early days of the pandemic, the administration issued a little-known public health statute called Title 42, which allowed the president to quickly deport people and turn away asylum seekers based on a health emergency. COVID-19 qualified as just such an emergency.

Now, as we write this introduction on May 11, 2023, the day Title 42 is scheduled to end, the nation once again has been submerged into a media-driven panic. Our relatively new, 24-hour-a-day, seven-day-a-week media cycle amplifies crises, both real and imaginary. Some Republicans in the United States accuse the Biden Administration of adopting an "open borders" policy with regard to immigration from the global south. The administration has been attempting to police a 1,900-mile border while adhering to long-established principles, laws, and practices—including acknowledgment of the right of people fleeing unimaginable situations abroad to seek refuge in the United States as per 1980 law.

Four nations of Latin America—three of which we cover in this book—have been designated by the Biden Administration for special treatment due to difficult socioeconomic/political conditions in those nations. They are Nicaragua, Venezuela, Haiti, and Cuba. Americans are shown images of poor people at the border, or in border cities such as El Paso and Brownsville, Texas, and the media profits by scaring Americans with a false narrative that the nation is being overrun, or flooded, with immigrants from the global south. Nothing could be further from the truth, and current immigrant numbers as a percentage of the US population are lower now than they were in 1910. The big change of course involves the "origin" of immigrants. Sixty-four years ago, in 1960, 84 percent of immigrants living in the United States were born in Europe or Canada. The Immigration and Nationality Act of 1965 ended the "quota" system for immigrants and adopted a "skills" system that emphasized family unification, and aligned with the nation's newer, more modern approach to civil rights. It opened immigration to the United States from every corner of the globe; thus, in 2018, 75 percent of all immigrants to the United States were from Mexico, other Latin American nations, plus Asia. Not white people. This change in origin—from Europe to Latin/Asian—combined with the 24-hour news cycle has contributed to the anxieties, fears, and focus on immigration in recent years—a sort of unique "American Hysteria" to borrow from Professor Román's title outlined above.

What is, then, the proper number of immigrants to be absorbed into the US economy? No one knows the answer to that question, but recent labor shortages in the United States, during and after the pandemic, suggest that we have yet to reach an equilibrium concerning number of immigrants needed as our national economy grows and the native-born American population ages. This seems like a particularly "utilitarian" approach to immigration; the reality, though, is much more complex, and the United States has a well-earned reputation as a place of refuge for folks arriving here from inhospitable places. Such places include Haiti, which as of this writing has no functioning government after the President was mysteriously assassinated in 2021. Cuba, which has suffered under a US-imposed embargo since 1961, has been unable to prosper economically, in large measure due to US policy.

Why these nations?

We selected seven nations—but we could have chosen more. We decided to focus on nations that are relatively proximate to the United States, and all of the selected nations have had long histories of interactions with the United States.

Mexico is our first nation of interest: of the approximately 45 million foreign-born folks living in the United States as we write, about 25 percent of that total come from Mexico. Mexico is significant to the United States given the historic ties and struggles—and shared border—between the two nations. Of course, much of the story is adversarial: in 1846, the United States invaded Mexico and took 51 percent of Mexico's national territory in what came to be known as "The Mexican-American War." Mexicans refer to this war as "the War of North American Aggression." The war was settled when US troops agreed to leave Mexico, the United States paid Mexico $15 million, while adding 30 percent to the national landmass. This treaty, known as the Treaty of Guadalupe Hidalgo, is a landmark treaty that has defined modern relations between the two countries.

Despite this mid-19th-century setback, Mexico today is the 14th largest economy in the world, a major oil producer, and the United States' largest trading partner, as of late 2023. The North American Free Trade Agreement (NAFTA) treaty (1994) permanently tied our society (and Canada) to Mexico in terms of economic, trade, manufacturing, and other concerns.

There are seven Central American countries, but one, Belize, was colonized by the British. People there speak English, and Belize falls out of the academic parameters of "Latin American Studies" even though it clearly falls within Central American territorial integrity. Guatemala and Honduras are included in this book, though we could have certainly included

El Salvador and Nicaragua. Those four nations have witnessed a preponderance of US intervention, particularly during the 1980s when civil wars raged in the region. The Guatemalan Civil War (c. 1960 to 1996) was particularly cruel; there were approximately 300,000 killed during that time, including documented cases of genocide, as adjudicated in a landmark 2013 ruling against former president Efraín Ríos Montt. He was convicted of genocide by a Guatemalan court, but that sentence was later vacated by the Guatemalan Constitutional Court. In 2018, a Guatemalan court found the Guatemalan army responsible for committing genocide against the Maya Ixil people. For writing candidly and clearly about this period of genocide in her own nation, Indigenous activist and witness Rigoberta Menchú Tum was awarded the Nobel Prize for Peace in 1992.

A long history of economic intervention, particularly in the agricultural sector, defines the US relationship with Honduras. The United Fruit Company was active in Honduras (and in other nations of Central and South America) and shaped policies and operations that undervalued workers/agriculturalists, stifled economic development and industrialization, and created a system for wealthy oligarchs to thrive—upheld by a majority poor population. In 1998, Hurricane "Mitch" devastated the nation and much of the Caribbean coast of Honduras was destroyed. Hondurans living in the United States (mostly in Los Angeles and New Orleans) were offered TPS—Temporary Protection Status—which continues for those Hondurans who qualify (about 60,000); however, the Trump Administration attempted to end TPS for several nations and was supported by a 2020 2–1 court ruling. One of President Biden's first acts as president was to extend TPS to people from many nations, including Honduras, Haiti, and Venezuela (as well as El Salvador and Nicaragua).

Next, we focus on Haiti. This nation has led the list of poorest nations in the Western Hemisphere for some time and has struggled through natural disasters of biblical dimensions and equally devastating man-made political crises: The latest man-made crisis was the murder of the sitting president in 2021, a crime that has yet to be resolved. Significant Haitian communities are found in New York, Boston, and Miami, and we hope to more fully understand how the Haitian people have been influenced by TPS and other asylum protections. We also want to know how the relationship has evolved between Haitians confined to the Caribbean nation and those living in the United States. Haitians (and others) living abroad remit about \$3.1 billion (in 2022) to Haiti, 80 percent of that sum originates in the United States. Remittance payments account for about one-seventh of Haiti's entire GDP, calculated at \$20 billion in 2021. We will also study the historic markers that have shaped the Haitian story—a story widely influenced by multiple US military and other interventions.

Cuba's complicated story with the United States dates back to the mid-19th century (to the Ostend Manifesto) when the United States essentially tried to buy the island from Spain for $20 million. The United States imposed, effectively, a protectorate over the island nation in the immediate aftermath of Cuban independence (from Spain) in 1898. A 1959 revolution led by Fidel Castro and friends altered the relationship between the two neighboring nations, and in 1962 President John F. Kennedy imposed an economic embargo that, to this day, still prevails. Cubans who arrive in the United States are generally treated with special consideration under the 1966 Cuban Adjustment Act, which recognized the economic and political hardships imposed by the Castro dictatorship. The embargo, the continuation of "Revolution era" policies, the collapse of the Soviet Union in 1991 (which had provided significant financial aid to the island), and of course COVID-19 have all conspired to create great hardship for the people. As recently as spring 2023, Cubans have been selling their possessions to purchase air tickets to Nicaragua; from there, many have made the long, harrowing journey up through Honduras, Guatemala, and Mexico to seek asylum (or Parole) at the US border.

Venezuela's precarious political situation began in 1999 when Hugo Chávez emerged as the leader of the oil rich, OPEC nation in northern South America. When oil prices were high, in the early 2000s, Venezuelans enjoyed Chávez-directed largess; a 2002–2003 strike of oil workers was designed to bring down the Chávez regime, but it further consolidated his power. President Chávez died of cancer in 2013, and his successor, Nicolás Maduro, was heavily sanctioned by the Obama and Trump administrations for widespread corruption and anti-democratic practices. The Biden Administration, in late 2022, began to relax restrictions, especially those dealing with PdVSA (the state-run Venezuelan oil corporation), given shortfalls in the US supply of crude as a "Russia" ban/embargo took hold in the wake of that nation's hostile actions against Ukraine. But the economic and political situation in the once-wealthy oil-soaked nation has led to a massive exodus in the past ten years or so. Approximately seven million have left, or about one-quarter of the population. Many have fled to neighboring Colombia, but others have literally walked to the border with the United States—seeking some sort of help. They have traveled through Colombia, through the Darién Gap—an inhospitable jungle separating Panama and Colombia—through Central America and Mexico, and on to the US border. In January 2023, President Biden announced that 30,000 people from Nicaragua, Haiti, Cuba, and Venezuela would be allowed in to the United States if they apply from their home nations, enter at a legal port of entry, and pass a background check. This policy, in theory, is designed to bring more order to the migratory process and prevent dangerous crossings through the Sonoran Desert with unscrupulous smugglers, or *coyotes*.

Colombia constitutes our seventh nation. Currently, in 2023, there is political stability in the nation of 50 million people but Colombian migration to the United States has followed similar "push" patterns seen in the other nations studied in this text. For example, during the 1980s, when drug lord Pablo Escobar seemed to be in charge of the nation, many fled the nation to nearby Miami and settled in Kendall, a western suburb of Miami with relatively low population density and affordable single-family homes. In the 1990s, the Colombian insurgency reached a critical point, with perhaps as many as 25,000 men, women, and children engaged in active combat against the Colombian government and an underfunded, frequently overwhelmed military. Many Colombians left during this time period, some seeking political asylum in the United States, others heading to European nations—especially Spain. Presently, there is political and economic stability in Colombia, though the nation is not at total peace. An armed insurgency known as the ELN is still actively engaged against the military, but the current president, Mr. Gustavo Petro, is dialoging with this insurgency group that dates back to the early 1960s. The real issue now (and in the past) involves creating a society that more equally distributes and shares the riches and resources of the nation. Colombia exports petroleum, coal, and other minerals, and is rich in agriculture, coffee, textile production, and light manufacturing. It is one of the most "unequal" nations in Latin America, and until there is greater harmony between economic production and wages/distribution, Colombians will seek a better life outside of the Colombian nation.

This book will help the reader understand the vast, complex, and multinational nature of immigration. Sound bites and talking points from television newscasters—whose salaries depend on our being frightened and tuning in for "guidance"—those are not the people who have the best interest of the general public at heart. We think a short, clearly written, historically driven narrative focusing on seven nations in Latin American that have, traditionally, sent people to the United States, is the best way to learn some of the "truths" about the immigration imbroglio. Voices too from the people who have made the journey, or who have been left behind, can help us understand this phenomenon.

A book on immigration—like this one—needs (by definition) to be updated periodically because the stories change constantly, but not necessarily substantively. In other words, throughout our history in the United States, there have always been people willing to come here based on difficult or impossible conditions back home. Not all immigrants to America came of their own free will: Obviously, enslaved Africans had no say in their capture and transport across the Atlantic Ocean. But the current economic climate in the Americas has changed dramatically in the past generation. The great recession of 2008–2009 gravely affected the world economy, and prices for exports traditionally sourced in Latin America (wheat, soybeans, oil, and other minerals, etc.) dropped. The economic situation improved by the mid-2010s but COVID-19 dealt the second blow to the world economy and affected not just economic development of the Americas, but political processes as well. Anti-democratic leaders such as Jair Bolsonaro in Brazil, who mocked mask mandates and suggested he might turn into an "alligator" from the life-saving vaccine, were pushed out of office. The same happened in the United States with Donald Trump and his less-than-coherent COVID strategy.

The interviews: Most of the interviews in this book took place during the 2023 calendar year. The interviews were in person, via ZOOM, and via telephone. We used a short, standard interview sheet, and interviews were conducted in Spanish and English, and responses were translated by the authors. We did not offer money for interviewees' time, except when asked; thus, in one case we paid the interviewee $50 for a half-hour conversation. Some interviewees preferred to respond in writing, via email, though we preferred to speak directly to the people who generously shared their stories with us. We were surprised to learn that many interviewees were uncomfortable using their names; thus, we've changed the names of all of our interviewees. We've mentioned this to show some of the tensions that exist in this nation between and among immigrant communities. There's an implicit "non-conversation" among those who are documented and those who are not and those in the intermediary space who are here with Deferred Action for Childhood Arrivals (DACA) protections or TPS.

We're producing this book to provide a new generation of students and other interested folk the opportunity to reflect on our nation's history, our nation's immigrant past, and to think about the future of immigration—or a future without immigration. While we certainly don't have all the answers to the immigration story, these seven stories, reflecting seven distinct nation's histories—connected to one larger nation to the north—is an attempt to refocus our attention on the people who migrate and who we often (in the United States) blame and demonize for wanting to come here—for wanting to try and improve their lives and the lives of their loved ones.

A note on our maps: Our seven maps were created using Shutterstock images for the seven nations. We've added in the capital city for each nation, plus the "air" distance from that capital city to the nearest US border. Given that many people can neither afford an airline ticket to the United States or the costs/fees associated with the VISA required to enter the United States, we've provided a sense of the challenges faced by those who cannot fly to an international airport in the United States. For instance, Cuba is an island, and the Caribbean Sea is a formidable border. Guatemalans often arrive in the United States overland from their homes, traversing Mexico by land, car, bus, and "*la bestia*"—the train. It's a long, brutal journey, and the maps are intended to show, or suggest, that arrival in the United States is a singular focus and obsession for many from our seven sending nations.

MAP 1.1 Colombia

DISTANCE TO US BORDER: 1,520 MILES

OBSTACLES TO TRAVEL TO THE UNITED STATES: VENEZUELA, DARIÉN GAP, CENTRAL AMERICA, MEXICO

Source: Captian.N/Shutterstock

1

COLOMBIA

In Search of the American Dream

During the 1920s, approximately 1,200 Colombians became "lawful permanent residents" of the United States. Seventy years later, that number jumped to more than a quarter million Colombians who have gained lawful residency. The disparity between those two statistics offers at least a preliminary explanation of a migratory process and story. US immigration laws changed substantially during that time period, and Colombian history/socioeconomic development left few options for people to expand their horizons. For many, the only suitable option was out-migration.

A Brief History of 20th-Century Colombia

Colombia has been—despite the media and Hollywood depictions—a fairly stable nation in South America that counts about 50 million people in 2023. The nation is rich in mineral resources (gold, coal, and oil, among others) and a variety of climactic ranges that allow for the growth of virtually all agriculture for human consumption. The nation is divided by three branches of the Andes mountains, which divide and "die out" in Colombia. The unique, complex geography has influenced the economic development of the nation, has made true integration of the nation virtually impossible, and has led to sociopolitical conflict and distrust of biblical dimensions. Colombia should not be—but often is—compared to nations with completely distinct geographies and cultures: Argentina, for example, or the United States. There are no easily accessible "Pampas" in Colombia, i.e., the vast open fields of Argentina that converted to a massive export trade of wheat, hides, and meat starting in the late 19th century.

DOI: 10.4324/9781003357605-2

Colombia suffered an especially embarrassing international indignity at the beginning of the 20th century when the Isthmus of Panama (a department or state of Colombia) was "separated" from the nation and declared independent. This action had the strong backing of the Unites States, which sought (and had been denied) permission by the Colombian government to build a transoceanic canal through Panama. This so-called loss of Panama created deep resentment in Colombia and essentially froze out diplomatic and cultural relations between the United States and Colombia for nearly a generation. During the 1920s "Dance of the Millions" (when the rich counted their fortunes in "Millions" of pesos for the first time), coffee accounted for 80 percent of the economy, and most of the Colombian product was destined for export to the United States or western Europe. The collapse of the world economy, precipitated by the Stock Market Crash in New York in 1929, had grave consequences for the export sector, but Colombia was able to rely more heavily on an internal domestic market and reoriented the economy toward light industrialization. Textiles and foodstuffs, bottled drinks, and houseware items were produced, and the economy gravitated toward a dynamic western city known for entrepreneurial spirit and efficiency: Medellín.

Political and economic disagreements—which essentially carried over from the mid-19th century—turned violent when landless *campesinos* faced off against landowners who reasserted control over their lands as commodity prices increased internationally in the lead up to the Second World War. This "conflict" never really resolved and essentially redeployed as an active insurgency in the early 1960s with the establishment of revolutionary groups, the Revolutionary Armed Forces of Colombia (FARC) and Army of National Liberation (ELN). The Colombian government, with an underfunded, undertrained, and unenthused military, could neither control the entire national territory nor provide protection to the people, large landowners, or urban and rural poor. During the early years of this insurgency (the 1960s), many middle-class people in the cities made the decision to emigrate because Colombia, for them, offered little in terms of future mobility or economic opportunity.

The 1980s and the onset of narcotics exports from Colombia ushered in a new period of violence and political upheaval in Colombia and accelerated the pace of out-migration. During the 1980s, about 105,000 Colombians received "permanent lawful residency" in the United States, and a "new" destination in the United States became attractive to Colombians: the sunny, open space of south Florida.

The late 1990s was a particularly painful period for Colombia. The economy went into a free-fall, especially after US sanctions were applied to the Colombian government. The 1994 presidential election was seen as "corrupted" when the president, Ernesto Samper, was shown to have accepted about $6 million in campaign funds from the *narcotraficantes*. The contraction of the economy at this time led to a serious recession in 1999. This, combined with an intensification of the FARC fighting force (some estimate the FARC forces at 25,000 men, women, and children in arms against the government at this time), suggested Colombia was heading for "Failed State" status. An infusion of funds from the United States at this time (the so-called "Plan Colombia") was designed to bolster the Colombian military with an initial $1.3 billion aid package. That funding has grown to about $11 billion, as of this writing in mid-2023.

Plan Colombia and the heavy-handed tactics of the administrations of President Álvaro Uribe Vélez (2002–2010) did in fact serve to corral the FARC, pushing them into extreme "corner" territories of the nation. The death toll to civilians, insurgents, and soldiers alike was very high—and a "false positive" scandal (where the military essentially murdered innocent civilians to falsely push up the tally of killed insurgents) soured the nation on the war. People in the nation demanded peace, and negotiations began in 2012, concluding in peace accords signed into law in late 2016. During this entire period—a 52-year war that extended from the early 1960s to the peace accords—Colombians felt victimized in their own nation, and the statistics released as part of the Peace and Reconciliation process indicated that about 450,000 people lost their lives during the insurgency and counterinsurgency. It should come as no surprise that about 10 percent of the Colombian population has "left" the nation—one of the highest percentages for a Latin American nation. Peace has not been perfect, or "total," in Colombia since the signing of peace accords with the FARC, and as of this writing it is estimated that about 1,500 insurgents remain dedicated to the ELN, which began fighting against the government in the early 1960s—inspired by the 1959 Revolution in nearby Cuba.

The "push" factors (i.e., the forces pushing people out of Colombia) might seem obvious given the narrative above, but Colombia's unique geography in Latin America explains this phenomenon further. Colombians were all but locked into their surroundings, particularly in the densely populated Andean regions. But with the advent of the 20th century, road construction to support automobiles and the airplane broke Colombians out of their isolation. It should come as no surprise that the first modern airline in the Americas is Colombian. SCADTA (Sociedad Colombo-Alemán de Transportes Aeréos) was founded by Germans living in the Barranquilla area of Colombia on the Caribbean coast. An early sort of Colombian "myth" involves the democratic spirit imposed on the nation by the westward expansion of rugged explorers, who founded and settled the city of Medellín. In short, Colombians have always been eager to defeat the constraints geography imposed on them. Migration to the United States from Mexico, which shares a 1,900-mile border with the United States, and Cuba, which is only 90 miles from Key West, Florida, is "easier," and so the Colombian migration out of the nation (the push factors) would coincide with technological changes and would track with sociopolitical realities and complexities during the 20th century.

The Panama problem, explained above, cast a pall over Colombia-US diplomacy, and normal relations did not return until 1922 via the Urrutia-Thomson Treaty. During this period, i.e., prior to, during, and immediately after the First World War, the Colombian elite—those who could travel abroad—preferred Europe, especially France and England, to the United States. The War essentially shut down travel across the Atlantic, and Colombians after the war began to view the United States more favorably, particularly after 1922. Europe, for all its cultural dynamism and singular significance in terms of law, economic development, and educational norms, was far away geographically, and the gradual shift toward the United States made sense from a purely practical point of view. In 1918, this attitude was firmly established by Colombian President Marco Fidel Suárez, who made his famous *Respice Polum* speech. The Colombian nation could only prosper, according to the South American leader, by attaching itself firmly to the "North Star"—i.e., the emerging and powerful United States.

The 1920s represented a period of prosperity in Colombia as demand for Colombia's primary export, coffee, rose. People from the middle class in the United States and Europe adopted an "upper class" habit, coffee drinking, with an added benefit: Caffeine allowed people to work longer hours, more efficiently, and gradually the habit of coffee drinking filtered down to the working class. During the 1920s, all of these factors benefited supplying nations, especially Colombia and Brazil in South America.

The significant "Push" factors—events unique to Colombia that pushed people out of the country and toward the United States—began in earnest in the 1930s as a variety of factors put pressure on the agricultural sector. First, of course, there was the global economic depression that affected demand for Colombia's main export at this time, coffee. Wealthy landowners abandoned their lands at this time—offering deeds (*escrituras*) and other benefits to rural workers, provided they took care of and maintained the property. Once economic prosperity returned in the latter part of the decade thanks in large part to demands for raw materials driven by the Second World War, poor people were pushed off the lands they assumed were theirs. Conflict ensued. And the conflict hasn't really ended—of course, Peace Accords were signed between the Colombian government and the FARC insurgents, but there are still active insurgent groups in the nation, and the Colombian military has never exerted complete control over the national territory.

People who had other options left the country. In the 1930s, very few Colombians migrated to the United States; according to data supplied by the Deptment of Homeland Security (2021 data), 1,278 Colombians obtained permanent residency status in the United States during the entire decade. That's about 120 people per year! This suggests that Colombians were not eager to leave their land during this time, and that the United States was not a popular destination. This makes sense given the enormity of the economic crisis in the United States during the first part of the 1930s, where up to 40 percent of the US population seeking employment could not find work. The policies of Democratic President Franklin Delano Roosevelt helped transform the US economy by pushing the "state" to become more involved in economic planning, pushing money into public spending projects—the so-called priming of the pump that would help generate work for people at this time. The onset of the Second World War in 1938 and planning/spending that accompanied that conflict helped stabilize the US economy. But the initial push factor, conflict, and limited economic opportunity in Colombia meant a mere trickle of Colombians to the United States during the 1930s.

A sort of "continuation" of this push occurred from this time onward and continues today. A day that lives on in infamy in Colombia is April 9, 1948. On that day—a sort of equivalent to the Kennedy Assassination in the United States, i.e., a day that changed the course of the nation's history—Jorge Eliécer Gaitán was assassinated on the streets of Bogotá. Gaitán represented the hope of a generation of Colombians who had been left out of decision-making and the economic prosperity of the nation; he was a typical populist leader in Latin America (he had been Mayor of Bogotá and was expected to win the presidential election of 1950), but unlike Lazaro Cárdenas in Mexico or Getulio Vargas in Brazil, he never arrived at the seat of power. His death sparked days of rioting, with sacking and burning of parts of the capitol city's downtown, and forced a hardening of mistrust between the established leadership and the "popular masses."

Nobel Prize laureate Gabriel García Márquez was in the city that day, studying law at the National University. The bleakness of this particular day, plus his dislike for the formality, cold climate, and general conservativism of Bogotá pushed him out of the city. He left for his native north coast (he went to Barranquilla) and never returned to the nation's capital.[1]

Colombians, sensing that something had broken on April 9, 1948, hunkered down for what would become known simply as "La Violencia"; basically, the nation moved through a ten-year, undeclared civil war that affected poor people in the countryside more so than urban dwellers. At the end of the "process" perhaps as many as a quarter million Colombians had been killed. A 1958 political agreement (called the National Front or Frente Nacional) paused the violence and kicked off a fairly successful power-sharing arrangement between liberals and conservatives—two groups that had been fighting for over a century.

The push out of Colombia was dramatic during this time. During the 1940s, 3,500 Colombians secured legal residency in the United States; from 1950 to 1960 that number jumped fivefold, to about 15,600. There's yet another fourfold increase in outward migrations from Colombia during the decade of the 1960s—from 15,600 to over 65,000. Of course, these are official numbers and do not reflect people who arrived in a clandestine manner or people who decided to overstay tourist visas. But the 1960s represented a real period of change for Colombia since two serious armed insurgency groups emerged in the nation. One remained in arms until 2016, and the other (the ELN) still remains active as of this writing in mid-2023.

The reasons for the "insurgency" date back to the unresolved land issues—from the 1930s—discussed above. But another driver of the armed insurgency involved the general condition of Latin America during this time period. The Cuban Revolution in 1959 animated a generation of young university students and the emerging middle sectors in Latin America who felt locked out of both economic prosperity in the region and political participation. The ELN, which emerged in 1964, was directly tied to the neighboring revolutionaries to the north. Specific to Colombia, a general amnesty was offered to insurgents in the so-called llanos orientales or eastern plains of the nation; President Gustavo Rojas Pinilla organized a demobilization of this group in the early 1950s, and offered amnesty in 1958. But the governments post-amnesty developed a sort of amnesia, and poor people continued having their lands encroached upon while the rich used the national army as their battering ram. People got fed up, and in 1964, the government attacked poor people at "Marquetalia" in the coffee-growing area of the Department of Caldas and sparked conflict.

People decided to leave Colombia at this time, as noted above in the dramatic upswing in migration. There was little confidence in the "institutions" of Colombia and the military was a very weak, reactionary "barracks" military with limited formal training. Their training would increase, substantially, thanks in large part to funding provided by the United States. Plan Lazo was a sort of "Cold War"-inspired military assistance program designed to go after and destroy communists in the region—or anyone that seemed communistic or might one day be swayed by communist rhetoric. So, as the killings ticked up again, people in Colombia—after having survived the ten-year "Violence" (c. 1946–1958)—decided things might get worse rather than better. They left.

The 1960s represented a time of collaboration between the United States and Colombia, at least on the surface. The Kennedy Administration warmly embraced Colombia's commitment to democracy and the club of smart, university-trained economists who understood economic development on Chicago, not Havana terms. Colombia was sort of the "darling" of Kennedy's Alliance for Progress—a program that offered economic development to nations in Latin America that were democratically inclined, willing to follow Washington's lead, and committed to stable, incremental free-market economic development. Kennedy, in fact, traveled to Bogotá in December

1961 to launch "Ciudad Techo"—a middle-class neighborhood on the western edge of the city that would be renamed, after the President's death, as simply "Kennedy."

But when the 1970s began, a cruel confluence of events occurred that affected the Colombian economy. First, funding for the Alliance stalled out; the Alliance essentially collapsed shortly after Kennedy's death (and the ouster of democratically led governments in Peru, Argentina, and, in 1964, Brazil). Kennedy's successor, Lyndon Baines Johnson, was more interested in a domestic "Great Society" than an overseas Alliance. Second, overproduction of coffee meant a flattening of the price of coffee internationally, which affected Colombia negatively. In 1970, coffee exports accounted for approximately 40 percent of export earnings at this time. Finally, the oil shock of 1973 negatively affected the economy of Colombia—a nation emerging as an important producer of petroleum, but not nearly as important as neighboring Venezuela or Mexico to the north. Colombia's petroleum output was not significant enough to affect world market prices at this time, and the nation was still a "price taker"—forced to follow the trends of the international market rather than set or establish prices.

The economy, then, never really "took off" in Colombia—it sort of flattened out, and people in Colombia, particularly the middle classes who wanted more from life than a minimum wage job, limited access to quality education, and the inability to own their own home, decided to move on. The United States became a destination of choice at this time.

No one knows exactly when cocaine production and export from Colombia became part of the socioeconomic reality of the nation, but the bitter feud, the massive amounts of ill-begotten wealth, and the murder of high-level government officials, especially the young, dynamic Minister of Justice Rodrigo Lara Bonilla, who was gunned down in 1984 on orders from Pablo Escobar, ushered in a new phase in the national conflict. War had been declared, and it would last for about a decade, until Escobar himself was killed in late 1993 on a rooftop in Medellín. About 106,000 Colombians received lawful permanent resident status in the United States during the decade of the 1980s, a tremendous increase from 30 years prior.

The 1990s pushed people out of Colombia due to a confluence of factors: First, the continuation of the drug war violence; second, an increasingly bold and well-financed insurgency (through kidnapping and extortion and protection of the drug lords); and finally, the onset of a "neoliberal" model of economic development, favored by the nation's "accidental" president, University of Los Andes economist César Gaviria Trujillo. Gaviria was a true believer in the efficacy of the neoliberal model, which is sometimes referred to as the Washington Consensus and declared (among other things) that state intervention in economics always leads to inefficiencies. In practical terms, the 1990s represented a giant "fire-sale" in Latin America as governments sold off (state-run) telephone networks, utilities, mining enterprises, and airlines. Private capital flowed in to buy up these entities, and massive layoffs ensued not just in Colombia but throughout the region. This constituted yet another "push" factor and indicated to Colombians the difficulty of achieving a decent livelihood in their homeland, particularly for the middle and working classes. This, combined with the deteriorating security situation and an unenergetic response from the ruling elites (who could, after all, pay for private security and lived in relatively safe neighborhoods in the northern sector of Bogotá or the southern sectors of Medellín), pushed people out of Colombia and toward the north.

The first couple of years of the 21st century represented a dramatic change in Colombia. Between 2000 and 2002, three major events came together to challenge the collapse that largely characterized the previous decades. First, the US Congress authorized a massive, mostly military aid package in order to "save Colombia"—the authorization amounted to about $1.3 billion, making Colombia (at the time) the third most favored nation (after Israel and Egypt) concerning US aid. The deal was pushed through by President Bill Clinton, who enjoyed an excellent personal relationship with Colombia's president, Andrés Pastrana Arango.

Next, a semi-serious peace process collapsed in early 2002 when the leader of the FARC, Manuel Marulanda, left the president of the republic, Pastrana, sitting alone and sweating in a previously agreed-to meeting place in the Colombian jungle. It was an embarrassing rebuke to the president, the government, and the peace process, and from there things fell apart further. Shortly after this tragedy, an unorthodox politician (he was from neither the Conservative nor the Liberal Party) was elected president in 2002. Álvaro Uribe Vélez offered a plan to completely destroy the FARC and all other insurgents. He presented himself as an indefatigable patriot who would stop at nothing to end the insurgency. The billions of dollars (now, 24 years after Plan Colombia, the United States has supplied about $11 billion in mostly military aid to the Andean nation) helped professionalize and modernize the military, and the FARC forces were in fact corralled and pushed into the corners of the nation.

But the decade of 2000–2010 was characterized by all-out war on all fronts. The paramilitary forces—private armies that murdered with gusto, never completely constrained by the army or government—committed almost unimaginable massacres, though they did finally demobilize in the "Ley de Justicia y Paz" of 2006. Though President Uribe, reelected to a second term in 2006, provided Colombians with a sense that the government was regaining the upper hand, the price and collateral damage of the war was felt everywhere. One example, the so-called False Positive Scandal rocked the nation in 2008. The government was "caught" in a murderous plot designed to demonstrate to the world that the army "kill" numbers were much higher than they actually were. It was a scandal made in Vietnam some 40 years earlier, when the US army inflated the body count of killed "VC" (Vietcong) in order to continue an unwinnable war. In Colombia, thousands of young people were taken from poor neighborhoods in Bogotá and elsewhere; they were executed, dressed in the clothes of guerrilla insurgents, and photographed as evidence of "battlefield successes."

Naturally, with so much chaos during this decade, more than a quarter million people left Colombia to seek legal residency in the United States. The next decade, 2010–2020, can be viewed as a decade of transition to peace. Peace Accords were finally signed with the FARC in 2016, and the nation is currently grappling with the challenges of ending a war that dates back to the early 1960s, perhaps even the early 1930s.

But Colombians continued their out-migration, and as many as five million Colombians live outside of the nation, or about 10 percent of the total population. The "Peace Process" of the middle part of the 2010 decade did not result in a "return migration" to Colombia, as Colombians, who had been leaving for decades, established residency, citizenship, and household economies in other places, including of course the United States. A total of 186,000 Colombians left the nation during this "Decade of Peace," but that number represents a reversal from the prior decade when 237,000 left. Colombians—the majority who leave—tend to travel (80 percent of all migrants) to four countries: neighboring Venezuela and Ecuador, Spain, and the United States. However, the recent (2017 to present) socioeconomic collapse in Venezuela and strict restrictions placed on the economy by the United States have made Venezuela a net exporter of people, which will be the subject of the final chapter in this book. By some accounts, Venezuela has lost (to migration) about 7 million of its population of 30 million, which suggests the intensity of the economic crisis there. Approximately 2.8 million Venezuelans have migrated to Colombia during the past six or seven years.

What has pulled people from Colombia to the United States? Colombians, since the beginning of the 20th century, have been attracted to the United States as a place of innovation, modernity, and civil liberties, with a strong dedication to democracy. For many Colombians, the United States has also been seen as a place where people can get ahead economically without reliance on *apellido* (family name) or religious/political party affiliation. Colombian society is strongly tied to local concerns and regional matters. Given the complexity of Colombian geography, travel "abroad" was nearly impossible until the advent of modern modes of transportation in the early part of the 20th century. Part of the "pull" then is the relative geographic proximity of the United States to Colombia, and a sense that the United States is more spacious, open, and free. People—particularly wealthy Colombians—began sending their children to the United States rather than Europe for education, especially as the two world wars made travel and prosperity difficult in many sectors of Europe.

Education has been an important "motivator" for Colombians to visit the United States. For example, in 2012, 161 Colombian nationals were granted the degree of Ph.D. at US universities, ranking Colombian number 13th in the list of most doctorates earned (by foreigners) at US universities. So, the university has been an important "pull" for Colombians hoping to advance through education. Up until 30 years ago or so, Colombians were "forced" to leave their nation if they hoped to earn a Ph.D. in History—for example. The first doctoral program began some 30 years ago at the National University in Bogotá. Many of the Colombian professors earned advanced degrees in Europe, and increasingly, after about 1990, in the United States.

Another important "pull" toward the United States was the socioeconomic stability for "most" people (not all) in the United States during the decade of the 1950s which contrasted so sharply with the Colombian sociopolitical reality of that decade. In Colombia, the 1950s is the decade of "La Violencia" when neither the elected governmental officials nor the officials under their command in the armed forces were able to control the entire nation. Some have argued that the president, at this time, controlled little more than the "Plaza Bolívar"—the National Plaza directly north of his residence, the Plaza that houses to this day the Congress, judiciary, city government, and the Roman Catholic Cathedral. At this time, in the 1950s, the alliance between the United States went from hostile (early in the century) to collaborative: The best example of such collaboration came during the Korean Conflict (or War) when Colombia, under the semi-fascist leader Laureano Gómez, sent troops to Korea—the only nation in Latin America to do so. About 5,000 Colombians served in Korea between 1951 and 1954.

Colombia was rewarded handsomely for its participation in the conflict. US military figures, including President Dwight D. Eisenhower, saw Colombia as a reliable partner in terms of advancing US interests abroad. Military equipment and funding flowed to Bogotá, and the security interests of the two nations would only grow stronger over the next seven decades.

The 1960s represented a decade of significant pull by the United States—for Colombians and other immigrants. In Colombia, frequent economic downturns, an economy that seemed geared to promote the prosperous, crumbling public schools, and a sense—dating back to colonial times—that folks were "locked" in their socioeconomic station, which contrasted sharply with the "American Dream." Elmhurst, Woodside, and Jackson Heights (Queens) New York were the destinations of choice for Colombians, along with Puerto Ricans, and people from Southeast Asia. [White] New Yorkers were fleeing these sections of Queens for Long Island and the Jersey suburbs during the tumultuous days of the 1960s in America.

Regular airline service, it should be noted, began in 1946 between Bogotá and New York; DC-4, four engine propeller airplanes, covered the route on "Avianca," but only the wealthy could afford to fly—a reality that did not really change until the 1990s when airlines in the United States (and world) "de-regulated" and prices fell dramatically.

Real estate in Queens, New York, was inexpensive in the 1960s, and many opportunities were to be found in construction; public schools in New York were enviable at this time and—perhaps more importantly—they were free for all. Many Colombians from the middle sector of society migrated to New York at this time and established a strong Colombian presence in Jackson Heights that remains viable to this day.[2]

Finally, a fifth "pull" factor involves the explosion of American culture at this time and its impact in Latin America generally and Colombia, specifically. American music—particularly jazz, blues, and music associated with the African American struggle in the United States —was popular among the urban elites. Elvis Presley, who could be seen on television and heard on radio, represented the sort of youthful energy of the American nation. American cinema at this time—and the overall impact of Hollywood—defined a cool, sunny California vibe. Sears Roebuck opened in Colombia in 1951 and offered a distinct "American style" shopping experience. Taken together, these pull factors helped convince Colombians from all strata of society, with the exception of the rural and urban poor, that new opportunities awaited them in America and that the nation was open for eager, hardworking Colombians who merely had to tolerate the English language and harsh winters of New York. With patience, a little luck, and in solidarity with other Colombians in New York, many Colombians found the American dream viable during this time period.

Some Laws: The 1965 Immigration Reform

President Lydon Baines Johnson signed a new immigration reform law in 1965. The law was designed to harmonize the nation's aspirational ideals with the reality of the times. In other words, the United States could no longer, in the era of focus on Civil Rights, discriminate against immigrants seeking a better life in America. Most agreed, by the 1960s, that the 1924 Reed-Johnson Act (our first comprehensive immigration law) was discriminatory in that it set "quotas" based on racist assumptions from the early 20th century. By Johnson-Reed, numbers favored (for immigration purposes) people from northern European nations, plus England, Scotland, and Ireland. In other words—white people. The Immigration and Nationality Act of 1965 did away with the 1924 law and opened up the United States to people from every corner of the world. Now, after 1965, quotas disappeared, and people were allowed in based on specific "skills" needed for the US economy and society. Visas were attached to certain categories—student, agricultural worker, etc.—and the new policy was concerned with family unification and reunification. Thus, Colombians were able to join family members who had made the journey to the United States in the 1950s and early 1960s, and the new immigration policy was a tremendously attractive piece of legislation for Latin Americans and others hoping to restart their lives in America. Open competition based on talent, determination, and skill was a "better" message than the previous system, based on outdated and outmoded quotas.

In 1980, the United States committed to a modern asylum system. A law was signed in that year by President Jimmy Carter in reaction, to some degree, by the crises in Vietnam and Central America: war, military dictatorships, abuses of basic human rights, and people fleeing for their lives. People literally, "Who run," to borrow a line from a popular song, "into the arms of America."[3]

But America didn't really have the capacity (or will) to receive modern immigrants; even at the time of the European Holocaust, the turning away of a European vessel, whose lights could be seen off the coast of Miami, terrified people throughout the world. Many of the people on board were returned to Europe and executed in Hitler's death camps. They were seeking refuge in America. In 1939, the *S.S. St Louis* left Europe with 900 German Jews aboard, seeing safe passage in Havana. Their ship was denied entrance to Cuba and sat off the shore of the United States, where the captain sought permission to land. He appealed directly to President Franklin D. Roosevelt but was denied permission. The ship returned to Europe, where about 200 of the innocent passengers were killed by the Nazis.

This story is not well known by US citizens as it clearly contradicts the image (or self-image) of the United States as a nation willing to accept those literally running for their lives. The first refugee act was passed in 1948 as a way to support people fleeing Europe at this time, and an asylum law was passed by congress in 1979 and signed by President Carter in 1980. The law added language, universally accepted, defining refugees as people able to demonstrate a "well-founded fear of persecution" in their native nation based on political, religious, or ethnic standing. The 1980 law was at least partially a reaction to the situation unleashed in Vietnam, after an 11-year US military presence there and the collapse of Saigon in South Vietnam in 1975. Americans felt obligated to take in as many people from that "communist" country as possible.

People from Central America and Colombia took advantage of this situation as their nations—especially Nicaragua, El Salvador, and Guatemala—were torn apart by civil war during this period. Much of the mayhem was financed by the US government, or via schemes cooked up in the White House—the infamous Iran-Contra scandal, which helped fund the opposition group (the *contras*) in Nicaragua, was a major scandal during the second Reagan Administration (1984–1988). With regard to Colombia, about 280,000 Colombians arrived as legal permanent residents between 2002 and 2012, and of that number 16 percent, or 43,000, arrived as refugees. This was a particularly difficult period for Colombian nationals, as the new administration of Álvaro Uribe promised not less but more war, and his policies created great internal dislocation and out-migration. Colombia, it should be noted, has one of the largest, if not the largest, internally displaced persons crisis in the world, with an estimated seven million people officially displaced due to the violence and mayhem of the past 50 years or so. Most of those people are displaced "internally."

Carla Fuentes's story[4] is somewhat typical of how Colombians manage to arrive, and remain, in the United States. Carla, born in Bogotá, is an 80-year-old professor at a university in the United States; she began teaching as a teenager in her hometown immediately upon graduation from "Normalista Superior," a type of high school designed to train teachers. At that time, some 60 years ago, the Jesuit University in Bogotá offered night classes, and Carla taught during the day and studied history at night there, at the Pontificia Universidad Javeriana. Via a program called "Operation Amigo," she first visited the United States as a high school student in the time period immediately after the Cuban Revolution; this program was promoted and patronized by the Miami newspaper *The Miami Herald*, and Carla spent a month visiting and studying at Palmetto High School in South Dade County (Miami). She lived with a family "in a mansion" and knew, at that time, that she wanted to return to the United States.

Ms. Fuentes earned her BA degree from the Javeriana (in history) and decided to compete for a scholarship, which she won, to study in the United States at the University of Texas, Austin. First, she spent six months at Brattleboro, Vermont, to focus on English language skills; with the MA degree in hand, she was asked to teach courses in history at both the Javeriana and the Universidad Nacional de Colombia in the nation's capital.

The next step was a return to the United States to complete her Ph.D. in history—again at the University of Texas. After completing her Ph.D. in 1993 on a student visa, she returned to Colombia and took a research/administrative position at the U. Nacional. Thirteen or 14 years later, after being shot through the hand in a bank robbery, she decided to return to the United States and was offered teaching positions at two colleges. She's been living in the United States ever since and became a naturalized US citizen about ten years ago.

Leena Del Barrio's story is similar in that she, too, is a scholar and a teacher who lives and works in the United States.[5] Born in Bogotá about 50 years ago, she came to the United States (to New York state) at the age of five with her mother and grandmother and attended public schools in New York.

Prior to arriving in the United States, she knew about the country "since I regularly watched *I Dream of Jeannie* on TV and I knew they spoke a language there called English." As a teenager, she applied for and was authorized to have a "Green Card"—a sort of first step in the process of securing citizenship. Green card holders are allowed to work but cannot vote. Given that Ms. Del Barrio was a dual citizen (Colombian and Swiss—her mother having been born in Switzerland), she applied for citizenship as a Swiss citizen, which at the time was "easier" than applying as a Colombian. Because her mother obtained US citizenship when Leena was a minor (at age 17), she did not have to take the citizenship test. "We were lucky," said Ms. Del Barrio, "to have a good family friend who was a lawyer and he helped us out with the process, so I didn't have to dig too deep into the system."

Leonardo Cienfuegos is 66 years old and came to the United States to pursue a graduate-level education here, after having obtained his law degree in Bogotá, Colombia.[6] He worked as a lawyer but decided to come to the United States "to improve my professional profile and advance my academic preparation, while gaining significant international experience." Eventually, Leonardo was able to obtain a green card (permanent residency in the United States) after marrying his wife, a US citizen. Currently a professor of journalism at a south Florida university, Mr. Cienfuegos is one of many examples of people who leave their native homelands due to the abundance of educational opportunities in the United States.

Danny Villa is a college student, age 20, born in the United States to Colombian parents.[7] Both his parents are from Bogotá, and he's been there a few times. He grew up in the Atlanta suburbs; his parents came to the United States "because they wanted a better life and to take advantage of educational opportunities in the USA." Danny's father completed a master's degree in computer science and has since returned to Colombia; Danny is here with his brother and mother. "We live in Marietta (GA), which is predominantly Black and Latino." He recounts how his grandmother married "a white guy in the US military"—a US citizen—and thus was able to procure a green card. This document, and his grandmother's status, facilitated the transit of his parents to the United States, and both boys (Danny and his older brother) are taking advantage of higher education in the United States. Danny plans to study computer science at a small college in the south, and his older brother completed a degree in public health from Tulane University in New Orleans.

Álvaro Suárez came to the United States in 1965. "I managed to arrive here via a family member who married a citizen of the US." He was born in Tolima, Colombia, and grew up in the capital of Eastern Plains, the *llanos*, Villavicencio. He was drafted to Vietnam and, upon return to the United States, lived in New York in a community of many Colombians, Jackson

Heights, Queens. He worked in the American bureaucracy for a while before dedicating his career to art—he is now known for his artwork and lives in the southwest United States. "Migration is what we do as human beings and animals," explained Mr. Suárez. "People who migrate illegally, or undocumented, feel a good deal of shame – and they often times prefer not to talk about their experiences as migrants." All migrants share one common feature: "We're all ultimately looking for home and acceptance."[8]

Conclusion

Colombia, a nation of some 50 million, has witnessed its fair share of tragedy and conflict over the past one hundred years or so. A significant escape valve involves "out-migration," and approximately 10–11 percent of the Colombian population live abroad; there are Colombians living in every corner of the globe, but the United States, and neighboring Ecuador and Venezuela, have been historic points of attraction for the Colombian people. Colombian immigration surged in the 1960s as a confluence of factors emerged: First, a slow-moving insurgency developed, and anemic national governments and an underfunded military apparatus meant that the insurgency metastasized. This, together with slow, uneven economic growth, pushed Colombians to look for better futures elsewhere. When the United States committed to a more pluralistic, democratic immigration system in 1965, many Colombians took advantage of the new law (Immigration and Naturalization Act, 1965) and came to America. They continue to do so to this day.

Notes

1 This story is told in *Living to Tell the Tale*, the author's autobiographical work published in 2004 in English. The book released in Spanish as *Vivir para Contarla* in 2002.
2 See Michael J. LaRosa and Germán R. Mejía, *Colombia: A Concise Contemporary History* (Lanham, MD: Rowman and Littlefield Publishing Group, Inc., 2017), chapter 11.
3 See the 1986 album *The Joshua Tree* by U2—specifically the song "Bullet the Blue Sky.".
4 We've decided to change names to keep anonymity for the interviewees who either spoke to us or responded to a survey. Most requested that we change their name for this project, and, for consistency, we've decided to change all names to protect the interviewees and their friends and family. Carla spoke to us (in person) in February 2023.
5 Ms. Del Barrio responded via email questionnaire in early 2023.
6 Mr. Cienfuegos responded via email interview form in April 2023.
7 Danny Villa spoke to us via phone from Atlanta, Georgia, on June 22, 2023.
8 Interview on January 3, 2024, in Tucson, Arizona, with Mr. Suárez.

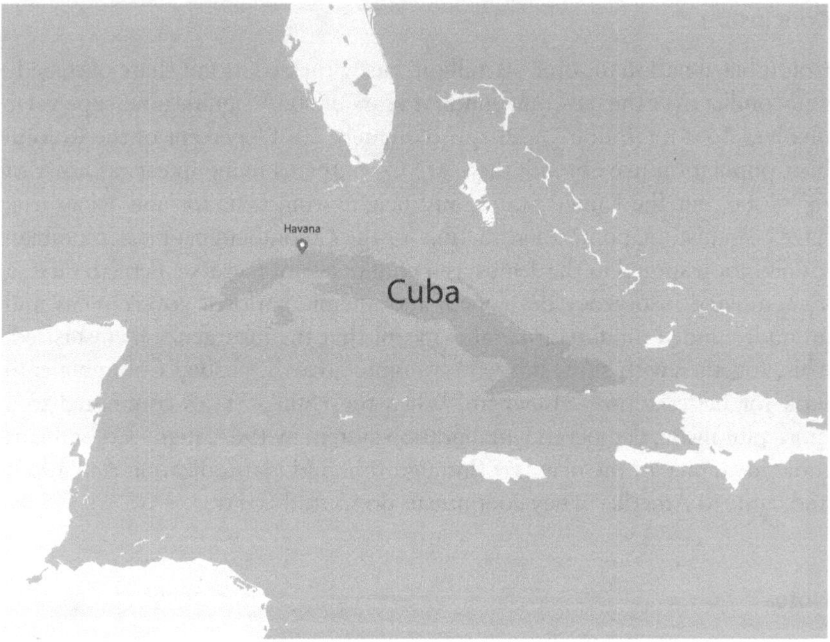

MAP 2.1 Cuba

DISTANCE TO US BORDER: 90 MILES

OBSTACLES TO TRAVEL TO THE UNITED STATES: CARIBBEAN SEA

Source: Captian.N/Shutterstock

2

CUBA

Economic Embargo, 63 Years On

Cuba has long been the subject of fascination for the United States. In 1854, the United States tried to buy the island from Spain for $130 million in what's known colloquially as the "Ostend Manifesto." The 35 years prior to this date witnessed a massive expansion of the continental United States. First, Andrew Jackson led an incursion against the Seminole peoples in Florida, waged war with Spain, and forced what's euphemistically referred to on many maps as "the acquisition of Florida" by 1819. Then, in 1846, the United States waged war with Mexico and acquired about one-third of the current continental United States—including Texas, New Mexico, Arizona, Colorado, and California.

Sadly, the motive for the 1854 interest in the island that sits 90 miles off Key West, Florida, has to do with the institution of slavery. The "Compromise of 1850"—with its backward-looking "fugitive slave law" provision—set up for an eventually larger conflict over slavery. Based on the passions aroused over this 1850 legislation, Southern plantation owners and others strongly suspected that slavery would not last forever in America. Thus, the turn to Cuba.

Christopher Columbus arrived in Cuba in 1492, and the native population, Ciboney, Taino, and others died of displacement and European-derived disease: smallpox, mumps, measles, and whooping cough, among others. Father Bartolomé de las Casas, a Dominican priest from Spain, was one of few Europeans to speak out about what he called "the Devastation of the Indians."

Santiago de Cuba, Trinidad on the south coast, and Matanzas plus La Habana on the north constituted the early cities and trading posts. Cuba

DOI: 10.4324/9781003357605-3

was a critical colonial acquisition in the Spanish overseas empire and served as a sort of "entrepôt" for the Spanish fleet, which would arrive there from Spain with European goods for wealthy colonists in the Americas, and return to Spain with bullion, silver and gold, and agricultural products. Since there was neither gold nor silver to be found on the island, Cuba for centuries (until it became an important producer of sugar cane in the 18th century) was a sort of "warehouse/trading post," with an impressive colonial culture, architecture, and a large contingency of royal administrators and officials (i.e., male Spaniards).

Independence, which arrived in the Americas in waves, beginning near Boston in 1776 and extending to about 1826—at the final battle of Ayacucho in Peru—eluded Cuba. The island was far from the main campaigns of revolutionary activity and solidly "royalist" in terms of structure and personality. There were wealthy Spaniards, loyal to the King and the overseas colonial project; by the early 19th century, Spaniards and mestizos lived with hundreds of thousands of enslaved people on the island of Cuba. Cuba became a major Caribbean producer of sugar in the late 18th century and early 19th century; Cuba's rise as a sugar producer coincided, roughly, with the collapse of the Haitian sugar economy after the conclusion of the Haitian Revolution in about 1804.

Spain tenaciously held onto Cuba—for both practical and cultural/historic reasons. But the ties between Madrid and Havana began to fray once, as described above, the United States's influence in the "Americas" grew. That growth, especially after 1848, was explosive.

Ostend in 1854 never came to fruition (i.e., US purchase or annexation of the island), and the United States Civil War, shortly thereafter, refocused recalcitrant southerners on reestablishing slavery elsewhere. If the 13th Amendment to the US Constitution prohibited slavery on US soil, southerners would turn their gaze south—specifically to Brazil, where a colony of Southerners reinstituted slavery. There, these so-called Confederados brought American-style plantation agriculture to a place where slavery was legal—until 1888. In Cuba, slavery would end about 1878 at the conclusion of what is known as the "First Cuban War of Independence" or the "Ten Years' War"—a brutal campaign that lasted ten years and did not, in fact, result in Cuban independence. The war did destroy the "Latifundia" system (large, landed estates dating back to colonial days) and resulted in the formal end of slavery on the island. Independence leader José Martí framed, to some degree, his political and literary aspirations around this conflict; he was jailed, exiled, and beaten by Spanish authorities for his deep commitment to Cuban autonomy. The hatred that emerged between Spaniards and Cubans left a space for "Americans" to move in and fill the middle space, which they did through investment in land and infrastructure, and by more fully integrating the Caribbean island into a growing network that articulated Havana with Key West, Tampa, Mobile, and New Orleans. Sugar, bananas, and tobacco (luxury goods at this time) were generating handsome profits for merchants all along that trade route.

Vicente Martínez-Ybor was a Spaniard and cigar manufacturer in Cuba who moved much of his operations to the United States in the late 1860s as "The First" war took form. He initially set up in New York City and Key West, Florida, but found an ideal location on the west coast of Florida just north of Tampa. That neighborhood is now referred to as "Ybor City." There, he set up a cigar manufacturing business and brought in laborers from Cuba, as well as managers and others who were anxious to leave Cuba during the war.

"The Second War" of Cuban Independence took place between 1895 and 1898. Early in the conflict, the Cuban patriot, writer, intellectual, and exile José Martí (he lived in Mexico, Guatemala, and New York City) was executed by Spanish forces. This compelled Cubans to fight with great ferocity to avenge the death of their martyred hero, Martí. It also drew the attention of the United States which, by 1898, had about $50 million invested on the island. The United States and Cuba used "tariffs" to essentially influence policy; the United States focused on Spain's growing cruelty in the conflict and had grown weary of European influence in what it perceived as its own "hemisphere." However, Americans were quite sanguine about the prospects of "Cubans" gaining independence, given that much—as many as 40 percent—of the officer Corps of the Cuban Rebel Army were men of color—Black and mixed-race men.

In 1898, the United States, under President William McKinley and his Secretary of the Navy Theodore Roosevelt, essentially invented a pretext to enter this conflict, and United States' presence on the side of the Cuban rebels proved decisive. Spain gave up in a matter of months, and a peace treaty was signed in 1899, the Treaty of Paris.

Before the US army left Cuba in 1902, it forced the signing of the Platt Amendment, which was attached to the Cuban Constitution of 1901. This amendment formally tied the United States to Cuba; American officials deemed Cubans as too immature to undertake the difficult work of establishing democracy on their own, so the Platt Amendment offered to help. The amendment authorized the United States to intervene militarily, economically, and politically (at any time). It also set up a permanent American presence on the island, the US Naval Base known as Guantánamo.

So, by the very earliest days of the 20th century, Cuba had in fact traded its colonial status (attached to Spain) for a new status of "semi-independent" or (for those who closely read the Platt Amendment) virtually no independence at all. The portentous words of Martí, late in the 19th century, had come true. The revolutionary leader asked, viewing US ambition suspiciously, "Once the United States comes in, who will get her out?"

During the first decade of the 20th century, about 44,000 Cubans immigrated to the United States. The long history of investment on the island by the United States, the trade links that had been established, and of course the proximity to the United States all favored migration north. The difficult independence situation (with Cubans essentially trading out one overseas master, Spain, for another, the United States) led inexorably to political instability on the island, and the United States again intervened militarily from 1906 to 1909.

Sugar production tells much of the story of Cuba's history during this time. About 1910, a worldwide shortage played to Cuba's strengths as a long-term sugar-producing nation. Restrictions imposed by the First World War helped Cuba, since the price of sugar rose, and the linkages to the US market were clearly established. Sugar consumption grew during this time in the United States, and, though the price crashed in 1920, it regained strength, and by 1928 sugar was trading at record high prices. With the collapse of the international economy in 1929, the price of sugar, a few years later, had declined by about 60 percent. The island's second leading export, tobacco, fell by $30 million, from $43 million (in total exports) in 1929 to $13 million by 1933.[1]

In 1924, Gerardo Machado was elected president but remained in power until 1933, ruling at the end in an arbitrary and dictatorial fashion. With a subsequent rise in the price of sugar during the 1920s, Cuba's fortunes seemed unlimited, until the crash of the late 1920s. A "sugar quota" was established in the early 1930s to help regularize the flow and price of sugar from Cuba—the quota was designed to create political stability on the island as well.

However, with the election of US President Franklin Delano Roosevelt in 1932, a new relationship, in name and deed, developed between the United States and Latin America. The "Good Neighbor Policy" meant that the United States would no longer intervene militarily in Latin America (particularly in the Caribbean where intervention had been frequent), and "new" arrangements would help secure the stability of the Pan Caribbean region. Concerning Cuba, the first was the total abrogation of the Platt Amendment, which was replaced with the Cuban-American Treaty of Relations in 1934. The US Naval Base at Guantánamo would remain as part of the "legacy" of the 1901 amendment, and political stability would be ensured via support of a dictator, Fulgencio Batista, who ruled the island from the early 1930s through the arrival of Fidel Castro in 1959.

The Push Factors

It might seem obvious that the "Cuban Revolution" of 1959 was the primary push out of Cuba for many Cuban citizens. But long before the arrival of *los barbudos* [the bearded boys] in Havana, Cuba's history, political structure, and economy pushed people away from the island. Five factors are considered below in greater detail: First, the late 19th-century political upheavals leading to an independence from Spain that never really resulted in political independence; second, the influence of the United States in Cuba's socioeconomic development in the very early days of the 20th century; third, the political instability of this time period, which included military interventions by the United States; fourth, the limited nature of the Cuban economy, based largely on a mono-crop export structure; and fifth, a long-lasting, cruel dictatorship (Batista) which lasted until 1959, followed by a Revolution and a "different sort of" dictatorship in the form of the Castro Brothers.

The First War of Independence, which ended in 1878 and ended the institution of slavery, gravely affected the agrarian sector of Cuba. Sugar production fell, as did tobacco harvesting and manufacturing of cigars. Louis Pérez writes of 35,000 cigar workers without work; they migrated to "the expanding cigar centers in Key West, Tampa, Ocala (FL), and Jacksonville."[2] The cigar workers, it's important to note, are the sort of "intellectuals" of the Cuban labor force. Their tedious, artisanal work at desk allowed for "educational" opportunity in the form of "lectors," who would read books and newspaper articles to the cigar workers—who, until about 1930, rolled cigars exclusively by hand. Cigar workers were at the vanguard of labor movements. They were aware of workers' struggles in other parts of the world, and many were influenced by anarcho-socialist and/or Marxist/communist ideas. In other words, they were not afraid to migrate to places where there was more work to be found, where laborers had more and expanding rights and where society was "younger" and more open. Many moved to the United States at this time. Pérez suggests that about 100,000 Cubans left the island during the last third of the 19th century. About 55,000 of these emigrants went to the United States.

Cuba, it should be noted, attracted substantial immigration from Spain during the first third of the 20th century, i.e., in the Independence period. Cultural ties and an expansion of the sugar and tobacco and light manufacturing and Cuba's unique location between Europe, Latin America, and the United States made it an attractive destination. Many Spaniards had affective ties to the island, as well as relatives and land/and or businesses. Moreover, 600,000 Africans arrived, enslaved, during the 19th century, as well as about 130,000 Chinese contract workers, many of whom made a permanent home in Havana, particularly in the neighborhood known as "El Barrio Chino" or Chinatown.

But, during the time of independence, the United States's meddling in the economy and society, plus Marine Landings in 1906, 1912, and 1917, forced people out of Cuba. The Marine landings were in response to political troubles on the island. But, in fairness to the Cuban people, neither Cuban colonial status (until 1898) nor US-style-colonial status under the Platt Amendment really prepared the Cuban people for progressive, modern political rule.

Another "Push" factor out of Cuba involved the turbulent economic climate during the first third of the 20th century. Tens of thousands of Cubans fled the island at this time, using familiar patterns of immigration to Florida, New York, New Orleans, and other places in the United States. The Cuban economy suffered from a continual (dating back to colonial days) reliance on one or two agricultural products to sustain the economy, and when prices fluctuated or tastes changed—or other actors got involved in producing sugar or tobacco—the fortunes of Cubans declined. The First World War and the Great Depression (1929) were significant events that caused major disruptions to the Cuban economy, an economy that couldn't easily transition to either manufacturing or other agricultural production.

A fourth push came from the Batista dictatorship: Fulgencio Batista essentially ruled Cuba from the early 1930s to the eve of the 1959 revolution. Supported by the United States for his strong anti-communist stance, Batista ushered in a tourist industry and understood how he could benefit by promoting tourism, gambling, cheap rum, and tropical sunshine. Havana became a sort of playground for American upper- and upper middle-class tourists. In fact, 160,000 tourists from the United States visited Cuba during the winter months of 1948 and during the summer; about 40,000 Cubans visited Miami—according to a data compiled by Florida International University Green School of Public and International Affairs.

But the dictator pushed people off the island, and as Batista grew increasingly erratic and violent during his reign, Cubans left. For example, during the 1950s, there was a threefold increase in the number of Cubans leaving the island—heading to the United States, where they received permanent resident status, according to Department of Homeland Security statistics compiled in 2021 in their *Yearbook of Immigration Statistics*.

The biggest push factor was, of course, Fidel. The arrival of the revolutionaries in Havana on January 6, 1959, surprised the international community, but not necessarily the Cuban people. The revolutionaries had been waging a slow, deliberate campaign from east to west—toward Havana. The dictator had jailed and exiled Castro and his revolutionary collaborators, but when Fidel returned to Cuba from Mexico aboard the boat called *Granma* in December 1956, Batista claimed that all the "subversives" had been captured or killed. Batista's version was quickly dispelled when a journalist from the *New York Times*, Herbert Matthews, conducted a series of interviews with Fidel from the "Oriente" mountains, and the interviews were published in the newspapers in February 1957. Fidel was very much alive, together with his brother Raúl and Argentine physician/revolutionary Ernesto "Che" Guevara.

The revolution took advantage of a stalled economy, political corruption, institutions that didn't represent or reflect the will of the Cuban people, and a cruel tyrant backed by the US political and economic establishment. Fidel marched into town and was greeted enthusiastically by most Cubans—including the middle class in the city and professionals. The wealthy were weary from the beginning, and by the end of the first year of revolution (1959), landowners began leaving; as the revolution consolidated, professionals (agronomists, engineers, doctors, and dentists, among others) began to flee. Hundreds of thousands (at least 202,000 arrived officially in the United States) left Cuba during this first decade of revolution.

The Pull Factors—those forces that tugged Cubans toward the United States—might seem clear by now. The most obvious pull factor is sheer geographic proximity. Cuba is close to Haiti, Mexico, and Jamaica, but it's also about 90 miles from Key West, Florida. Cubans have been more attracted, historically, to the United States than to their Caribbean neighbors, though many Cubans live in Mexico—a nation that shares a similar culture, history, and language. As of 2016, there were 22,000 Cubans officially registered in Mexico, but most agree that that number is a low estimate of the actual Cuban community living there.

Another pull factor, in addition to geography, is simply the intense focus of the United States, dating back to the mid-19th century; the United States has long been interested in the island for strategic reasons and as a place of economic investment/opportunity. The United States investment of some $50 million on the island at the time of the "Second" war of independence (1895–1898) clearly pulled the island, metaphorically at least, toward the United States.

Another factor that drove Cubans toward the United States was the cultural dynamism of the neighbor to the north, and the links established through tourism; the American jazz scene attracted Cuban musicians. New Orleans and Havana were tied together, and transportation between the two cities was easy and relatively inexpensive in the early 20th century. Cuban boxers were successful in the United States at a time when "outsiders" were able to succeed in the boxing arena; Italian, Irish, Jewish, Black, and Cuban boxers came together to compete, and significant sums of money circulated around these competitions.[3]

But the Revolution of 1959 is probably the biggest pull factor. The United States seemed especially (and personally) displeased with the new Cuban path to independence. The "Monroe Doctrine" of 1823 had guided US policy toward the region since that time period: essentially, the United States declared in the early part of the 19th century that it would have de facto control over the region. The Cuban Revolution dramatically disturbed that tenuous balance, and the United States became, immediately, the patron saint of the opposition forces. This meant that the United States would assist Cubans who hoped to leave the island—hundreds of thousands of them during the first decade of the revolution.

There's also the Cold War to consider—closely tied to the information presented in the previous paragraph. At the conclusion of the Second World War, the United States emerged as the undisputed leader of the West with a clear, consistent anti-Communist and anti-Soviet Union message. Post-War organizations such as the United Nations, the OAS, chartered in 1948, and the Rio Pact of 1947, the Inter-American Pact of Mutual Assistance (a hemispheric defense initiative)—all pointed to the growing power of the United States. The OAS and Rio Pact specifically dealt with US leadership in the Western Hemisphere. Any nation with the temerity to go against the United States and its allies would suffer severe consequences. In Cuba's case, the rebellious nation was removed from the protections and assurances offered by these international organizations and agreements. Cuba was suspended from the OAS in January 1962. Fidel didn't seem to care all that much. In fact, in a speech at the Plaza de la Revolución (Havana), Castro denounced the OAS, referring to it as the "Yankee Ministry of Colonies and a military bloc against the people of Latin America."[4]

The final pull factor involves the strong communities established by Cubans in the United States, beginning in the 19th century. Cubans established themselves in Tampa, Key West, and later in Miami. They also lived in many places along the US East coast, especially in and around New York City. New Orleans, as a central Gulf Port, attracted Cubans due to business and trade associations and through the similarities in culture and climate of the two cities.

The pull factors are significant. Cubans came to the United States, and there are currently about 2.3 million Hispanics of Cuban origin living in the United States. No other nation comes close as a destination point for Cubans. Spain, with a 400-year history of "colonizing" the island (from 1492 to 1898), counts fewer than 180,000 Cubans.

US hostility toward the Cuban revolution was nearly immediate. President Dwight D. Eisenhower ended diplomatic relations between the two nations, and the incoming Kennedy Administration, in April 1961, authorized a failed invasion of the island that only consolidated Castro's position. Kennedy responded to this disaster with an economic embargo against Cuba—an embargo that exists to this day. Neither a military invasion, nor exclusion from the OAS organization, nor an embargo stopped Castro; the United States's low-frequency war against the tiny nation created a refugee crisis to which the United States responded with a variety of laws and policies.

Once military intervention and political operations failed, Cubans, who were opposed to the regime, realized that Castro and the revolutionaries were not going anywhere. An exodus ensued, and a well-known and documented operation was designed to bring unaccompanied children to Florida. "Operation Pedro Pan" [Operation Peter Pan] moved some 14,000 children during a two-year period from 1960 to 1962. They would be placed with family or other collaborative people living in Miami and would wait until they could be reunited with their parents.

Some funding was provided by the US government, and the operation was organized through the Roman Catholic Church. The Church was an early adversary of the Castro regime, since it had amassed considerable power, influence, and wealth on the island from its arrival there in the late 15th century. Most of the Pedro Pan participants were children and adolescents; most were male; and the entire operation was fueled by an anti-Castro hysteria telegraphed from Miami. Children were spirited out of Cuba as rumors spread that Castro would remove children from their families, cancel legal parental rights over children, and drop Cuban kids in "re-education" camps on the island. None of this actually happened, and the secret Pedro Pan flights—operated out of Havana to Miami via Pan American Airways—continued until all air service ended between the United States and Cuba. That occurred in October 1962 at the conclusion of the "Cuban Missile Crisis." Prominent Cuban-Americans arrived in the United States on these flights, including the educator Eduardo Padrón—past president of Miami-Dade Community College.

Perhaps the most significant immigration law to affect Cubans during this time period is a law written specifically for Cubans. It's the 1966 Cuban Adjustment Act (CAA), and it remains as policy in the myriad and complex cornucopia of US immigration law. The CAA is a follow-on legislation to the landmark national immigration legislation passed by Congress in 1965, which eliminated the previous era of "quotas" (enshrined in the 1924 Immigration legislation—the first comprehensive immigration act of our nation's history). In 1965, the government decided to focus on a "skills"-based immigration system and emphasized "family unification"—ideas more in concert with the mid-1960s focus on civil rights in a nation that had, up until the landmark *Brown v Board of Education* decision [1954], practiced legal segregation.

As the revolution rolled along in the early 1960s, people with some means (professional, middle, and working class) decided to leave and were offered protections by the United States (the CAA). This law, signed by President Johnson in late 1966, offered an "adjustment" or exception for Cubans. It put Cuba and Cubans at the center of the "Cold War" between the United States and Soviet Union; since the Soviet system of socialism began offering investment and the purchase of Cuban sugar in response to the US embargo and trade sanctions, the United States responded further by allowing Cubans who left the island Lawful Permanent Residency in the United States after a mere two years' residence in the country. The law, in 1976, was adjusted to require only one years' residence.

Clearly designed to show the benefits of capitalism over socialism, the CAA facilitated the regularization of migration documents for Cubans—and Cubans only—during this time, much to the consternation of other Latin Americans. But Cubans were treated differently due to the scope and depth of the revolution, a revolution the United States had no ability to modify. We could block trade, end diplomacy, and, at the same time, encourage Cubans to leave Cuba and live in America. From 1960 to 1970, the Cuban population in the United States grew from 79,000 to about 439,000. This number reflects the efficacy of the CAA.

The result of this act of Congress (it's still enforced to this day) is a rich, intense Cuban culture in and around the city of Miami and in other parts of the United States, especially Union City, New Jersey—or "Havana on the Hudson." Cubans have displaced throughout the nation, but Miami (South Florida) and New York/New Jersey remain strong centers of population and culture.

In 1962, María Eugenia Silla arrived in Miami (where she lives) from her place of birth in Matanzas, Cuba. She was three years old at the time, and she arrived by plane with her parents, grandparents, and brother. Her family was fed up with Fidel by 1962, and María Eugenia tells of an uncle "who had been in the mountains fighting with Fidel but returned to tell his family—and others—that the situation was screwed up [*muy mal*]; he described the whole situation as a giant fraud."[5]

She remembers very few details of her arrival in the United States as a three-year-old; Ms. Silla still recalls privation but credits the US government with helping arriving Cubans with food donations offered at the famous "Torre de la Libertad" in downtown Miami—the Freedom Tower. "They gave us butter and cheese blocks and powdered milk. We lived in a small house with about eight or ten relatives." Ms. Silla did not become a US citizen until she was in her 30s:

> My parents—who became citizens early upon arriving to the USA—didn't want me or my brother to become citizens; they were terrified that my brother, as US citizen, could or would be drafted into the Vietnam War. So, we waited until long after that conflict had passed.

Carlos R. Manuel, a painter and owner of a small business, is 65 years old and was born in Havana in 1958. Manuel left Cuba as an eight-year-old with his mother and father. Direct flights to the United States had ended by 1965, during which time Cubans could fly to either Spain or Mexico:[6]

> In Mexico, we lived in a small apartment and my father could buy cheese, and ham, and saltines! None of this was available in Cuba at that time and my parents never intended to stay in Mexico—and did not have proper papers to work there.

After a short time, they hired a *coyote* to take them to the United States.

> We left Mexico City with another couple and two men and travelled to the gulf – maybe to the city of Matamoros. Via the Gulf, we crossed into the USA on two rowboats, one of which tipped over. Everyone gathered in one boat, but all the luggage was tossed overboard to make room.

Mr. Manuel remembers the family stories of how his mother's small makeup case contained all the important family papers—including his birth certificate—and how the makeup and the papers were lost at sea.

Young Carlos arrived with literally nothing except the clothes on his back. They arrived in Miami after a flight from their landing area (probably near Brownsville, Texas) to Houston and from there to Miami, where it was difficult to determine the family's refugee status because no one had any papers. But sometime between March and May of 1966, they were accepted as refugees.

The family moved to New Jersey for a few years; Carlos's father was determined to make money and constantly worked:

> He worked at Hunt's Tomato Company during the day and as a dishwasher during the night. My mother—who had never worked in Cuba—found work in a New Jersey factory as a seamstress. She knew basic sewing but had never worked in a seamstress shop.

The family returned to Miami by 1970, where the father was offered some business opportunities. Carlos enrolled at a private Jesuit school, "Loyola Academy." He then attended college, first at a community college, and then he transferred to Florida International University (FIU). He was offered a scholarship to two law schools: Cornell in New York and the University of Miami in Coral Gables. He attended Miami but left after the second year: "I couldn't see myself practicing law so, ironically, I opened up a design and dress manufacturing business and my mother came to work for me."

Carlos's mother was flummoxed by this decision, and he recounts how she

> "worked for years as a seamstress so I could go to school – she didn't think it was a good idea that I became a seamstress, too—though I was also the designer and owner of the business. It all worked out in the end."

"Mariel" is the next significant immigration situation that occurred in Cuba. In 1980, a Cuban city bus was intentionally crashed through the gates of the Peruvian Embassy in Havana; soon, there were over 1,000 people inside the building (essentially on Peruvian sovereign soil) seeking some sort of escape from the oppressive conditions on the island. Shortly thereafter, there were 10,000 people at the Embassy, and the Cuban government retracted security. When Castro announced that anyone could leave out of the port of Mariel, a major immigration crisis ensued. Between April 15, 1980 and the beginning of October 1980, about 125,000 people left the island and arrived at the Florida Keys and Miami. This event was unfortunate, but both sides declared victory. Castro was able to push out many people he deemed undesirable (petty criminals, "homosexuals," people who didn't act in accordance with their gender, etc.) and the United States was able to prove that the socialist system wasn't working in Cuba—though few off the island were willing to admit to the outsized role of the US embargo and trade restriction in contributing to Cuba's misery. The city of Miami struggled to absorb so many people so quickly, but the myth that all "Marielitos" (people who left out of Mariel at this time) were hardened Cuban criminals is grossly exaggerated.

An international event that devastated Cuba in the early 1990s was the collapse of the Soviet Union in 1991. Since the earliest days of the revolution, the Soviets had supplied extensive funding to Cuba as well as a market for Cuban sugar. The Soviets benefitted from this relationship because it put them in proximity to their chief adversary during the Cold War, the United States.

The Soviets spent billions on economic development for the island nation and provided perhaps 750 million a year or more in military assistance in the early 1980s. They also massively subsidized the Cuban sugar sector. All of this, of course, ended when the Soviet Union collapsed in December 1991. This led to what's known as the "Special Period" in Cuba, characterized by shortages, hunger, deprivation, and misery for the Cuban people. That deprivation resulted from an estimated 35 percent drop in GDP during the first few years of the 1990s. In the summer of 1994, people began protesting and organizing makeshift flotillas [Los Balseros] using rafts, inner tubes, car parts—almost anything in an attempt to float away from the island.

None of this looked good for the Castro regime; Fidel Castro responded to the dissent with a bold but not particularly helpful "fiat" encouraging those who wanted to leave to leave. Thousands of Cubans attempted to escape via dangerous water routes in rickety homemade rafts. About 35,000 eventually arrived in the United States, and the chaos, drama, and danger of this period resulted in a new policy, called "Wet Feet, Dry Feet." President Bill Clinton's policy was designed to "not" encourage people from making dangerous sea voyages across the shark-saturated and storm-prone Straits of Florida. If Cubans were picked up in international waters (by the US Coast Guard or other military personnel), they would be repatriated to Cuba. If they, in fact, managed to land on US soil (dry feet), they would be admitted. The policy provided a "Cuban exception" to normal immigration policy, as it only applied to Cuban nationals.

President Barack Obama, some years later, ended this policy as one of the final acts of his administration in 2017. Obama and his family traveled to Havana in 2016, initiating a normalization in US-Cuban relations. While ending the problematic Clinton-Era Wet Feet Dry Feet policy, Obama policy sought to more fully harmonize Cuban immigration with "other" immigrants from Latin America and beyond. Cuba promised to receive repatriated Cubans, and the number of official visas (20,000) from the Clinton Era would be processed at the American Interests Section in Havana.

Donald Trump essentially reversed most of the Obama initiatives but President Biden, in January 2023, authorized a "Parole" program for Cubans, Haitians, and Nicaraguans. People arriving at legal entry points can be "paroled" into the United States after an interview, provided someone in the United States will receive them and support them (either a family member or friend).

Francisco Moreno told of his December 2022 travel to the United States. He left Havana, flew to Nicaragua (which authorizes Cubans to arrive to their country without a visa), and began the long march north.[7]

Moreno was a working musician in Cuba and earned the minimum salary of 3,500 pesos per month. "Remember, a carton of eggs costs 2,000 pesos." Moreno sold all of his belongings, borrowed money from friends in Cuba and in other places, and left on a flight out of Havana, arriving in December to Managua. Moreno recounts that "the flight cost 3,500 dollars," reflecting price gouging of poor people who have no other choice than to travel to that city in Nicaragua. He recounted a harrowing journey through Honduras "where the gangs, specifically the Mara Salvatruchas [MS-13], have more power and authority than the police, and they exact bribes from travelers." From there, he headed to and through Guatemala and finally up to the border with the United States, via the highway along the east coast of Mexico. "The west coast route is too dangerous, and it pushes people up along the east coast. People all along the route robbed us and the police took bribes."

After about three weeks of travel, including a crossing over of the Rio Bravo/Grande at Juarez, he managed to get "Paroled" into the United States; he only had with him his clothes (a hoodie and t-shirt) and was surprised at how cold Ciudad Juarez was in December. He could apply for residency in one year (as a Cuban) and citizenship in five years—assuming he obeyed the terms of his parole. He was unable to travel out of the United States during this time and could not visit his mother or other relatives who remained back in Havana. "If anyone asks if they should make the journey, I would tell them that it's very very difficult, but it's impossible for me not to encourage people to leave that system."

Cuba has captivated the imagination of the United States since at least the middle of the 19th century. Our immigration policies have offered a cut-out for people from the island of Cuba—a cut out that reflects basic Cold War principles and ideas. Helping Cubans leave a dictatorial island has been good for US prosperity and our image as a safe haven for democracy and freedom. But it forces us to ask: Is the Cuban government that much worse than the "non-existent" government in Haiti at the moment or the dictatorial slide of the Salvadoran government—where President Bukele is busy building a prison to house 40,000 Salvadoran "gang members"?

Normalization of economic and diplomatic relations with the island of Cuba is the only path forward. This will offer family reunification, easy travel between the United States and Cuba, and will benefit both societies. Our Cuba policy is still held hostage by the grudges and anger of old Cold War warriors. It's time to modernize the policy, free the movement of people, goods, and funds, and move out of the 19th and into the 21st century.

Notes

1 Louis A. Pérez, Jr. *Cuba: Between Reform and Revolution*, 2nd edition (New York: Oxford University Press, 1995), p. 253.
2 Louis A. Pérez, Jr. *Cuba: Between Reform and Revolution*, 2nd edition (New York: Oxford University Press, 1995), p. 100.
3 See David C. LaFevor. *Prizefighting and Civilization: A Cultural History of Boxing, Race, and Masculinity in Mexico and Cuba, 1840–1940*. (Albuquerque: University of New Mexico Press), 2020.
4 "Cuba and the OAS: The story of Dramatic Fallout and Reconciliation." By Stella Krepp. December 18, 2017. Woodrow Wilson Center, Washington, D.C.
5 This interview was conducted by telephone, on June 16, 2023, from Miami, Florida.
6 Mr. Manuel was interviewed, via telephone, on June 17, 2023, from his home in Tucson, Arizona.
7 Interview with Francisco Moreno, February 28, 2023—by phone, from Brooklyn, New York. Mr. Cody Stockton was on the call in New York and took/provided notes.

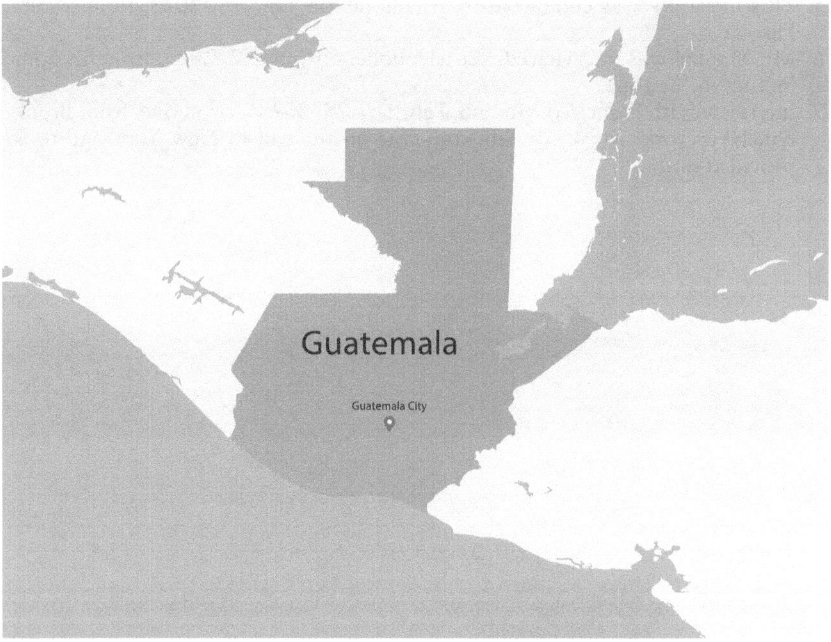

MAP 3.1 Guatemala

DISTANCE TO US BORDER: 905 MILES

OBSTACLES TO TRAVEL TO THE UNITED STATES: MEXICO

Source: Captian.N/Shutterstock

3

GUATEMALA

Looking to "El Norte"

In mid-2023, the son of the first modern, democratic president in Guatemala's history won elections that were viewed as free and fair by the international community. Bernardo Arévalo, the winner, is from the "progressive" side of Guatemalan politics, far removed from the recent trend toward corruption, collusion, and dishonesty that has characterized national leadership.

After the election, the ruling elite cried foul and did everything in their power to prevent the president-elect from taking office. But, as of this writing, Mr. Arévalo took office in early 2024—on January 16—in Guatemala City and has begun serving his four-year term. The installation ceremony was chaotic, as the opposition made a last-ditch attempt on inauguration day to stop the president-elect from becoming president, but they failed.

Eighty years ago, Mr. Arévalo's father, Juan José Arévalo was elected president of the same Central American nation and served as president from 1945 to 1951. He took over after the fall of the dictator, Jorge Ubico, who ruled during the turbulent days of the great depression and the Second World War. This "Club of Dictators" included some truly reprehensible people, such as the Somoza Family in Nicaragua (which came to control 40 percent of the national GDP before they were overthrown in 1979), the murderous Rafael Trujillo in the Dominican Republic, and Maximiliano Hernández Martínez, architect of "La Matanza"—the massacre—in El Salvador, which claimed the lives of about 2 percent of that nation's population in 1932.

Ubico, by contrast, was less lurid, but certainly no less dictatorial; he was elected in 1931 as "the only candidate" on the ballot and ruled with absolute

DOI: 10.4324/9781003357605-4

control from 1931 to 1945. The conclusion of the Second World War and the collapse of fascism worldwide left little space for Latin America's dictators to justify their anti-democratic rule, and many were pushed out of power.

Arévalo, the elder, was a philosopher and educator, and his political/social program was named "Spiritual socialism"—it was certainly fuzzy, but better than "Dictatorship," and people responded well to the change. Spiritual socialism implied a new relationship between the government and the people: the new president was committed to constructing schools, especially in rural areas that had been untouched by modernity. The new, more modern president planned to bridge a centuries old divide between the white/European conqueror class and the Native/Indigenous/non-Spanish-speaking people of Guatemala. This divide—which we can call classism, racism, internal colonialism—was and remains the crux of the Guatemalan problema.

The attempted coup by the wealthy/powerful Guatemalans in 2023 and 2024 is a sort of metaphor for the nation's 20th-century history. After Ubico fell, real reform began under Arévalo, and the reforms continued under his successor, Jacobo Arbenz, a colonel in the Guatemalan army. Arbenz was of Swiss/Guatemalan ancestry who built upon his predecessor's social programs but added an "agrarian reform" to the agenda. This reform infuriated the land-holding elite, though in reality it did little to directly affect their holdings.

But at this time, during the early days of the "Cold War," any program of agrarian reform in Latin America or the world was named Communism and sounded the alarm bells in Washington.

In 1954, Arbenz was overthrown in an operation staged by the Guatemalan elite with the help of the US State Department, CIA, and President Eisenhower. The Roman Catholic Church's Cardinal Spellman in New York City assisted as did leading clerics in Guatemala. Arbenz left the presidency by walking into the Mexican Embassy and asking for asylum. The new leader, Carlos Castillo Armas, a military officer approved by the CIA and Eisenhower Administration, ushered in a 42-year reign of terror, including civil war and genocide, from which the nation has yet to recover. Castillo Armas was assassinated in 1957, three years after the coup.[1]

Castillo Armas's first act as leader was to overturn the 1952 agrarian reform. Essentially, the reforms begun a mere seven years earlier under Arévalo's spiritual socialism had come to a dramatic end. The next phase of Guatemala's history—a civil war that began in 1960 and lasted 36 years—would take the lives of between 250,000 and 300,000 Guatemalans and included acts of genocide whereby entire communities of indigenous peoples were wiped out. People, if they could, began to flee this wholly human made tragedy.[2]

Guatemala is the most populous nation in Central America, with approximately 18 million residents. According to the 2020 US census, about 1.7 million Guatemalans live in the United States, and the economic impact of citizens living abroad is critical. According to data from 2021, about $15 billion flowed from "remittance" payments to Guatemala, mainly from relatives living in the United States. This money represented about 18 percent of the Guatemalan total economy—or GDP. Guatemalans primarily live in southern California, New York/New Jersey, and Washington D.C./Arlington, Virginia, area of the nation. Recently, Guatemalans have been moving to Florida and Texas—two states with low taxes, agreeable climates, and plenty of land.

Generational poverty, systemic racism against Indigenous communities, and state-sponsored repression have resulted in out-migration from Guatemala. The first military campaign against the Guatemalan people occurred in the 1960s, according to Handy, when the political ideas of Arévalo and Arbenz, and the popular political parties they built, were crushed under the weight of military regimes. These militaries were supported and oxygenated by the United States, which was fighting a three- (or more) pronged conflict: a general Cold War, a war in Vietnam, and a war against "subversives" in Latin America. In the wake of the 1959 Cuban Revolution, Guatemala became a key locale for "fighting subversives," and, hence, during a seven-year period from 1956 to 1963, "annual U.S. military assistance to Guatemala multiplied by ten times."[3]

Military assistance from the United States would continue, fueling much of the mayhem for the Central American nation. During a five-year period, from 2017 to 2021, the United States supplied about $66 million worth of military assistance to the so-called Northern Triangle nations of El Salvador, Honduras, and Guatemala. Guatemala has become, recently, a particular area of focus in the United States's attempt to stem the flow of migrants from Central America, to and through Mexico, and on to the US border.

Guatemala became the focus of the migration crisis when US Vice President Kamala Harris, on her first overseas trip as vice president, spoke in Guatemala City in June 2021. Her message was clear. "Do not come. Do not come," said Ms. Harris in comments that were widely derided in the United States and around the world. Her remarks were seen as a feeble attempt to "go tough" on immigrants, most of whom want to move north to secure a better life for themselves and their loved ones left behind. The comments were also completely contrary to the message inscribed on the Statue of Liberty in New York Harbor, penned by Emma Lazarus—a sort of generally understood, national mission statement of the United States of America: "Give me your tired, your poor, your huddled masses yearning to breathe free," wrote the poet, from her widely quoted 1883 poem "The New Colossus." Lazarus was a New Yorker from a well-to-do Sephardic Jewish family, active in helping Russian/Jewish migrants adjust to their new home (New York) despite deep prejudices and discrimination in America.

The Vice President's foray into the immigration morass represented a bad beginning for the administration, but clearly an improvement over the prior administration's (the administration of Donald Trump, 2017–2021) "Cage the Children" policy. The fact that immigration on the southern border remains an issue, which the Republican-controlled House of Representatives refuses to address, signifies the "issue" is centered squarely on US internal politics and power rather than helping poor people fleeing unimaginable crises back home, or protecting American workers and wages.

Why Guatemala

Guatemala matters in the immigration conundrum for at least two reasons: One, the intensity and brutality of the Civil War there from 1960 to 1996, which was mostly ignored (though emboldened through military aid) by the United States as it concerned itself with other more compelling foreign policy crises during this period, including Vietnam, the Middle East, "containing" the Cuban Revolution, Sandinistas in Nicaragua, and the fall of the Soviet Union. It literally took the writing—a sort of "Grito de Guatemala"—of the indigenous woman Rigoberta Menchú Tum to focus the world's attention on the catastrophic situation in her homeland. In 1983, a little over 40 years ago, she published her memoir titled *Me llamo Rigoberta Menchú y así me nació la conciencia*. In English translation, the book is widely referred to as *I Rigoberta Menchú*. For her efforts at exposing the chaos, the genocidal murder, and continual, historic harassment of indigenous communities in her native land, she was awarded the Nobel Prize for Peace in 1992. Menchú was the first indigenous woman to win the prize and only the second Guatemalan, after Miguel Ángel Asturias (who won for literature—author of *The Shark and the Sardines*), to win a Nobel.

Due in large part to her devastating, personal exposé of the socioeconomic/military situation in Guatemala, the world finally took notice. The United States, at that time, suffered from a bit of Central America obsession + fatigue. The Sandinista revolution in nearby Nicaragua (1979) captured the imagination of the nation—and the Reagan Administration—as Americans wondered if another "Vietnam" was developing shortly after America's biggest foreign policy failure in Southeast Asia. The news from nearby El Salvador was equally grim: there, the military (with the support of the United States), and groups affiliated with the Salvadoran military, willfully murdered the Catholic Archbishop Óscar Romero in 1980. Mr. Romero had called for an end to "the repression" and preached from the pulpit that "no soldier is compelled to follow an order contrary to the will of God," thus undermining military command and control authority. For that "crime," he was brutally murdered while saying mass in San Salvador. Then things got worse. On December 2, 1980, four US church women (three nuns and a lay missionary) were brutally raped and murdered by National Guardsmen, four of whom were convicted for the crime.

News of murdered nuns in Central America reverberated around the world: Peasant communities in nearby Guatemala being bulldozed into oblivion was less widely reported. This is why Ms. Menchú's work was so fundamental—it released in 1983, during the worst period of the state-sanctioned slaughter in Guatemala.

In March 1982, General Efraín Ríos Montt took over as leader of a military *junta*, and, from March 1982 to August 1983, ruled as a dictator. He had strong backing from President Ronald Reagan in Washington and—as a Christian Evangelical Pastor—stronger still support from Christian fundamentalists in the United States. About 70,000 Guatemalans were killed during this "scorched earth" campaign, and the military failed to distinguish between civilians and active *guerrilla* insurgents, characterizing nearly all indigenous people in the nation as "subversives." Nearly 300 native villages were completely razed during this time period, and some 700 were attacked or harassed by the military.

This is the context of both Rigoberta Menchú's work and the contemporary Guatemalan crisis. Naturally, people, if they survived, left their razed communities and either moved to the capital city or left for "el norte"—the North. Guatemalans were not treated kindly either by the United States or their Latin American brothers in the nation immediately to their north, Mexico. They were discriminated against due to their indigenous heritage; they were mostly poor people who had been accused of being "subversive," and their stories and reality hardly elicited sympathy from "officialdom" in either Mexico or the United States.

The Economy: Recent Trends

The Guatemalan economy is mixed and leading exports from the Central American nation are bananas, coffee, palm oil, and sugar. There is a significant textile industry, and "apparel" represents the leading Guatemalan import to the United States at just over a billion dollars per year. But inequality in Guatemala remains high with a Gini Coefficient of 48.3, putting it closer to Colombia and Brazil (at 54) and further away from Sweden, at 33.0. For context, a score of "zero" on the Gini represents absolute equality, and South Africa is considered the most overall unequal nation on the planet, with a Gini of 63.0.

Given such inequality across the board, "remittance" payments become significant in keeping people fed in Guatemala and represent about 18 percent of total GDP. This means, of course, that there is official "disincentive" to preventing out-migration as those who leave tend to head north, returning much needed capital to the country.

Guatemalans have not been supported by their government up until very recently. Mired in official corruption, they are not welcome in neighboring Mexico, and are denied, generally, the types of protections offered by the United States to Venezuelans, Cubans, Haitians, and Nicaraguans. The corruption in Guatemala has recently been noticed by the OAS. On September 1, 2023, the Organization of American States in Washington decried "efforts by the Public Ministry and other corrupt actors to suspend the President-elect's [Mr. Arévalo's] political party."[4] The government of Alejandro Giammattei (2020–2024) has recently been accused of corruption, and in the final days of his presidency Mr. Giammattei's government was rated as "good" by a mere 3 percent of the people polled. In January 2024, the US Department of State, citing clear evidence of corruption, barred the former head of state from visiting the United States. Naturally, all of this prompted people to leave, and in the final years of the Giammattei Administration out-migration increased significantly.

Natural calamities (Honduras), a lack of functioning government (Haiti), undemocratic regimes (Cuba), or political corruption (Venezuela and Guatemala) all push people from their nations of origin. But what makes Guatemala distinct? The people from Guatemala have not been designated for temporary protected status (TPS) or other types of much deserved considerations offered to Cubans, Venezuelans, and Haitians. Guatemalan's face other challenges in their attempt to immigrate to the United States: discrimination against indigenous Guatemalans—particularly those who speak neither Spanish nor English—has not been a friendly factor in their immigration journeys. Maya languages, it must be noted, are spoken by about 30 percent of the Guatemalan population.

The 1980s wars in Central America were widely covered in the media and were, in fact, the foreign policy predicament for the United States at this time: part and parcel of the larger "Cold War" with the Soviet Union. When the Soviet Union officially collapsed in 1991, it was time to reconsider the efficacy of all-out, brutal wars in Central America. First, Peace Accords were signed in El Salvador in 1993, ending the 14-year conflict that took the lives of some 70,000 citizens. Next up: Guatemala. A consensus emerged that neither the Unified Guerrilla Front nor the government could ever "win" there, so a push emerged to end the last remaining Central America war—Guatemala's longest and most deadly 36-year conflict.

In 1996, Peace Accords were signed, and part of the Commission of Historical Clarification (the official commission) required that a report, supervised by the United Nations, study the war and its wide-ranging consequences for Guatemala and its people. That report, titled "Guatemala: Memory of Silence," documented widespread acts of genocide committed against four Indigenous peoples in Guatemala including the Ixil Mayas, the Q'anjob'al and Cha Mayas, the K'iche Mayas, and the Achi Mayas. The report was released in 1999 and blamed 93 percent of the atrocities during the war on the government and 3 percent on the *guerrilla* groups.

A year prior to this report, the Catholic Church released its own report, a four-volume, detailed, and documented study of the atrocities. That report, titled *Guatemala: Nunca Más* (Never Again), was released in April 1998. Two days after the report's release, the chairman of the committee and a leading voice for human rights in the region, Bishop Juan Gerardi, was bludgeoned to death in his garage in Guatemala City.[5]

The reports clarified for the world, together with the work of peace activist and Nobel Laureate Rigoberta Menchú (discussed above), the Guatemalan 36-year tragedy, which might have begun in earnest with the United States' overthrow of the Arbenz presidency in 1954. In 2013, General Efraín Ríos Montt was convicted of genocide by the Constitutional Court of Guatemala. He was 86 years old and was sentenced to 50 years in prison, but died while awaiting a retrial on a procedural matter.

The Push Factors: In Context

Given the intensity and duration of the war—a war marked by genocide—the reasons why people would leave Guatemala are relatively clear. But one of the factors that makes Guatemala unique is the undeniable anti-indigenous racism that marked the behavior, for centuries, of the Guatemalan elite and their allies in the military, diplomatic sphere, and their friends in the United States. During the 1970s, about 23,000 Guatemalans sought Lawful Permanent Residency (LPR) status in the United States, but that number nearly tripled to about 60,000 during the cruel decade of the 1980s. During the 1990s, which saw the official end of the war but not the underlying conditions of racism, classism, and discrimination against indigenous persons, about 126,000 people sought lawful permanent residency in the United States. Many more Guatemalans made the journey to the United States as undocumented.

The Pull Factors to the USA

Guatemalans, as stated in the paragraph above, have been migrating to the United States for the past 60 years and longer. After the destabilization of the government—and overthrow of the elected president—in 1954 at the height of the Cold War, Guatemalans left for America and settled on the west coast and in the New York/New Jersey area. Like other immigrants from Latin America, New York at this time was in a transitory period. Space in the metropolitan area (including New Jersey) became available as people left for the suburbs, including Long Island and New Jersey during this period. Affordable rents plus good public schools, in addition to job opportunities, were attractive to Guatemalans fleeing political instability, racism, and a Civil War that had started in 1960 and showed no signs of abating.

A significant court case, *ABC v. Thornburgh*, affected Guatemalans and Salvadorans during the 1980s and helped solidify the reputation of the United States as a place that welcomed asylum seekers. The case originated in 1985 and was brought by various religious organizations that sought to protect Central Americans—specifically Salvadorans and Guatemalans—who were fleeing the horrors of their homelands. ABC stands for "American Baptist Churches"; simply stated, the lawsuit claimed that the neither the Immigration and Naturalization Service (INS) nor the Federal government were abiding by the Refugee Act of 1980—a landmark law signed by President Carter to offer those who could prove a "well founded fear of persecution" refugee status in the United States. The case was finally settled and nearly 300,000 Guatemalans and Salvadorans were offered an opportunity to reapply for asylum as well as gain a temporary protective status while their cases were under review. The case centered on the fact that the US government found it inconvenient to offer protection to the very people fleeing the flames of mayhem that it, directly and indirectly, had fanned.

This "case" resulted from (in large part) the US sanctuary movement that emerged at this time in and around Tucson, Arizona. In 1982, a Presbyterian church there declared itself a "sanctuary" where fleeing Central Americans could seek shelter, legal advice, and medical care. The movement spread throughout the southwest and exposed the hypocrisy of US policy: while the United States was funding brutal campaigns in El Salvador and Guatemala, that government essentially refused to acknowledge the effect this was having on the civilian populations there. The Reagan Administration's policies in the region were directly challenged by the sanctuary movement.

President Ronald Reagan visited Honduras in December 1982—at the height of Guatemala's scorched earth policy against "subversives" and described the president of Guatemala, Efraín Ríos Montt, as "a man of great integrity" and "totally dedicated to democracy."[6] Ríos Montt was convicted, we should remember, of genocide in 2013. The Reagan Administration was steadfast, determined, and dedicated to its policies in Central America: no pesky migrants, progressive religious people, or refugee seekers would cast shade on their policy. In fact, in 1983—at the height of the terror campaign unleashed by the military in Guatemala—one asylum seeker from that nation was admitted to the United States. That same year, 100 percent of all Cuban migrants seeking asylum were welcomed into the open arms of America. It's important to remember that Cubans lived in "Fidel Castro's Cuba"; Mr. Castro had challenged US hegemony in the region and was openly Marxist, whereas the leader of Guatemala, according to the sitting US president, was "totally dedicated to democracy." More than 10,000 Guatemalans were killed during the first three months of his government (which began in March 1982 and ended in August 1983), and over 400 indigenous communities were completely razed during his reign of terror.

The luridness of this period in history has proven fertile ground for writers of memoir and fiction. Rigoberta Menchú's book is widely cited and known, and another Nobel Laureate, Mario Vargas Llosa from Peru, has commented on the Guatemalan conundrum in his novel *Harsh Times*. Héctor Tobar, a Los Angeles writer and son of Guatemalan immigrants, has written widely on immigration as both journalist and novelist. Francisco Goldman—journalist and novelist—was born in Boston to an American father and Guatemalan mother; his journalism has focused on the murder of Bishop Gerardi (*The Art of Political Murder*), and his novel *The Long Night of White Chickens* was the inspiration for the 1997 John Sayles film *Hombres Armados—Men with Guns*. The film is a sort of pan-Latin American movie about murder, mayhem, racism, the military, corruption, and export economics in the region, but *Men with Guns* most closely tracks Guatemala of the 1980s.

Mexico, directly north of Guatemala, has not proven to be hospitable to Guatemalans fleeing north. Cultural factors, questions of nationalism, and poverty in the south of Mexico are all mitigating issues. "Programa Fronteras Sur" is an example of how Guatemalans have been treated by their neighbors to the north. In 2014, then Mexican President Enrique Peña Nieto launched this program with support and encouragement from the United States. Millions of dollars were applied to the program, ostensibly to protect Guatemalans and regularize their safe passage to Mexico, which shares a 750-mile border with Guatemala and Belize. More recently, the United States has attempted to essentially "outsource" its role as a destination for asylum seekers by seeking to strengthen Mexico's southern border.

This program, known to its detractors as "Wait in Mexico," was initiated by the Trump Administration and substantially upgraded through a dubious interpretation of a public health ordinance known as "Title 42," which allowed the expulsion of persons who had been in a country with the existence of a "communicable disease" and all but shut down the border during the COVID pandemic. President Biden has mostly kept in place Trump-era immigration policies, but "lifted" Title 42 when the pandemic emergency ended in May 2023.

Despite the funds spent on increased security measures and technology under Programa Fronteras Sur[7] and despite Mexico having apprehended more than 300,000 migrants in 2021, more than 20,000 people reached the border with the United States and ask for asylum. This number, of course, does not reflect the tens of thousands of refugees who reach the border and either cross illegally without apprehension or are apprehended and do not apply for asylum.

A confluence of factors has been especially unfavorable to Guatemalan migrants: First, Guatemala's corrupt Giammattei government (2020–2024) was unable to control criminal gangs or criminal activity in general, and so people left. Second, Guatemalans, for historic and cultural reasons outlined above, have not been especially welcome in southern Mexico—or in Mexico in general. Third, the United States has made few recent exceptions for Guatemalans despite grinding poverty, corruption, and gang activity. Guatemalans do not enjoy some of the special considerations offered to Venezuelans, Haitians, Cubans, or Nicaraguans.

Some immigration stories reflect this reality. Israel Cantor was born in Tajumulco in the province of San Marcos, Guatemala. He came to the United States in 2013. He was 16 years old when he arrived in Colorado Springs, Colorado, where he had relatives and was supported financially by his grandparents. His parents divorced, and he came north "because of crime and gangs; the police don't really investigate crimes, or help out very much...they only want money." Because of this, people tend to take the law into their own hands and retribution is widespread on the streets of towns and cities alike in Guatemala. "The gangs intimidate people and one tactic is to physically detain them, pour gasoline over the head and threaten to light the match ... it's very effective."[8]

Israel has been in the United States for a little over ten years and now lives in a medium-sized southern city. He's had trouble with attorneys—two of whom took multiple payments from him ($4,000 in one case, $3,000 in another) but provided very little in helpful counsel or practical assistance. Currently, he's waiting on a green card and has applied for asylum here in the United States. He was physically injured by gang members in Guatemala and fears for his safety were he to return there.

Like other interviewees in this book, Mr. Cantor spoke of the sacrifices made by immigrants. "I miss my family back in Guatemala—technology puts us in contact, but I can't give them a hug…it's a sacrifice." Mr. Cantor sends money, via wire networks, back to Guatemala, "but we're taken away from family and miss them and many people here say 'just return' but it's never that easy."

Cantor works at an Amazon distribution center—he received authorization to work here about three years ago. He also works at "odd jobs" in the city where he resides. Last October 2022, his son was born; Israel now lives with his wife, aunt, and son on the outskirts of the city.

People in the United States—if contemporary media reports are to be believed—have a difficult time understanding the immigration conundrum that faces the Americas. The case of Guatemala and Guatemalans is particularly complex and involves nearly 500 years of history. When the Spaniards conquered the territory in 1542, a long, slow process of cultural hegemony where white Europeans and their allies claimed to hold a superior culture, language, and religion was imposed (and their economic system) over the people of Guatemala and the region writ large.

Jim Handy views the arrival of Ríos Montt to leadership in Guatemala, via a military coup, as part of the fulfillment of the long history of consolidation of European values and traditions over native history and culture. He wrote how "the military [via the 1982 coup] was able to complete a process that began in 1542: the acquisition and control over the countryside and total breakdown of village autonomy."[9]

Rigoberta Menchú expressed the frustrations and despair of exile, just like Israel Cantor. She wrote, after fleeing Guatemala in 1981 as she was essentially being hunted by the army, "[T]he *compañeros* got me out on a plane to Mexico, and I felt a shattered, broken woman because I never imagined that one day those criminals would force me to abandon my country."[10] The complexity and difficulty of exile—whether via jet plane to Mexico or walking to the US border and arriving in Colorado—is equally traumatic for a Nobel Prize laureate as it is for an Amazon warehouse worker. People do not want to be pushed out of their homelands and living in exile, even if only for a brief period of time, is often a harrowing period in the lives of the travelers. But still, even the vast majority of those who were forced from their homes by unspeakable violence—as is the case of Ms. Menchú—prefer to stay at home. Writing about the people who helped her leave her native land in 1981, the Nobel Laureate wrote, "These people couldn't understand why, despite all the risks we run, we still want to live in Guatemala."[11]

"To emigrate is to die," said 19th-century Argentine intellectual Juan Bautista Alberdi, a man who was forced to live most of his life away from his native Buenos Aires. Americans, or people born and raised in the United States, have a mostly incomplete picture of the immigration equation given that this country (the United States) has been mostly a net receiver of immigrants from other places. There has not been civil or social conflict in recent times that has forced—or encouraged—people to leave the United States. The closest, recent example would be to focus on the young men who left the country during the Vietnam era, heading mostly to Canada, to avoid forced conscription for an extremely unpopular and mostly illegal war. That war was waged by the United States against a peasant society in southeast Asia, Vietnam. It's important to consider the totality of the immigrant experience: the factors that forced the departure from the native land, the journey itself, the people left behind and the nostalgia that builds over time. Guatemala's recent history (since the 1950s) offers an opportunity to understand more clearly why people leave a verdant, natural resource-rich land: they leave due to man-made warfare, man-made maldistribution of resources, and man-made racism, classism, and indifference to the plight of the people living within the same border.

Another story of immigration—the story of Nora de Baptiste—begins on the south coast of Guatemala, where Nora de Baptiste's family operated a plantation of rubber trees, an agricultural project introduced by the United States in the early 1940s during the Second World War; rubber, before it was made in a laboratory, synthetically, was made from the sap of the rubber tree, which grows in tropical climates. Brazil, Peru, Colombia, and Guatemala were some of the places in Latin America from where rubber was exported, and in Brazil and Peru vast fortunes were made during the early 20th century when the automobile became fashionable worldwide.

Nora spent her first 22 years in Guatemala but came to the United States after studying speech pathology at the Universidad Rafael Landivar. She followed in the footsteps of her brother who had moved to Mississippi to study at Mississippi State University; there, she was offered an assistantship to conduct language laboratory sessions at the University. One of the students in the course would, four years after her arrival in 1980, become her husband. "My future husband and I learned language—he learned Spanish, I learned English – by studying, and watching television and talking – we went to 'Shoney's' and talked."

"The farm was a fantastic place to live, and my life was pretty beautiful there, despite everything that was happening. We had fresh coffee, animals and other luxuries you don't have in the city." Eventually the family settled in Guatemala City for the educational opportunities there. After completing her university studies, as noted above, Nora arrived here and never returned full time to her native country. "It wasn't really the violence, which was terrible at that time, which pushed me to the USA," though the violence directly affected Nora and her family—her uncle "disappeared" from the farm one day and never returned.[12] Nora and her husband raised a family in Memphis, and she began teaching the Spanish language at the university level and recently completed about 16 years of full-time teaching before and during the pandemic.

Israel's and Nora's stories reflect two distinct realties separated by approximately two generations. But for people leaving violence, poverty, political corruption, or gang-related violence, the United States has been and continues to be the preferred place of refuge. Some, including Nora de Baptiste, have left Guatemala to pursue the many educational opportunities available in the United States. The opportunities here—for education or in fact for salvation—will always be present, and it's up to this generation of Americans, and the next, to make sure the doors for people like Israel and Nora stay open.

Notes

1 Published 40 years ago, Jim Handy's *Gift of the Devil: A History of Guatemala* remains the standard text for historians. For information on the American involvement in the overthrow of Arbenz, see S. Kinzer's *The Brothers*—a dual biography of the Dulles Brothers—Alan, Director of CIA, and John Foster, Secretary of State during the Eisenhower Administration.
2 In 1984, Gregory Nava released the critically acclaimed film "El Norte," which documented the migration of Guatemalans from their small Central American village to Los Angeles, California. Another film, made by the American John Sayles, dealt with the tragedy of Guatemala in a more allegorical fashion. "Men With Guns" was released in 1997.
3 Handy, *Gift of the Devil*. South End Press: Boston, 1984, p. 156.
4 See documents of the OAS, September 1, 2023, statement by Francisco O. Mora, U.S. Ambassador to the OAS.
5 See *The Art of Political Murder: Who Killed the Bishop*, by Francisco Goldman, 2008.
6 "Guatemalan Slaughter was Part of Reagan's Hard Line," by Greg Grandin. *The New York Times*, May 21, 2013 [updated].
7 The program was designed to support Mexico's ability to control migrants through it's southern border.
8 Interview with Mr. Cantor, February 11, 2023.
9 Handy, p. 255.
10 Menchú Rigoberta, *I Rigoberta Menchú: An Indian Woman in Guatemala*. (London: Verso, 1983), p. 242.
11 Menchú Rigoberta, *I Rigoberta Menchú: An Indian Woman in Guatemala*. (London: Verso, 1983), p. 244.
12 Ms. de Baptiste speculates that the army took her uncle away. He was working one day at the farm and some people passed through. He offered them water, and most likely was accused of collaborating with the insurgents. Such collaboration, real or imagined, often led to disappearance and death at the hands of the military or other extra official forces.

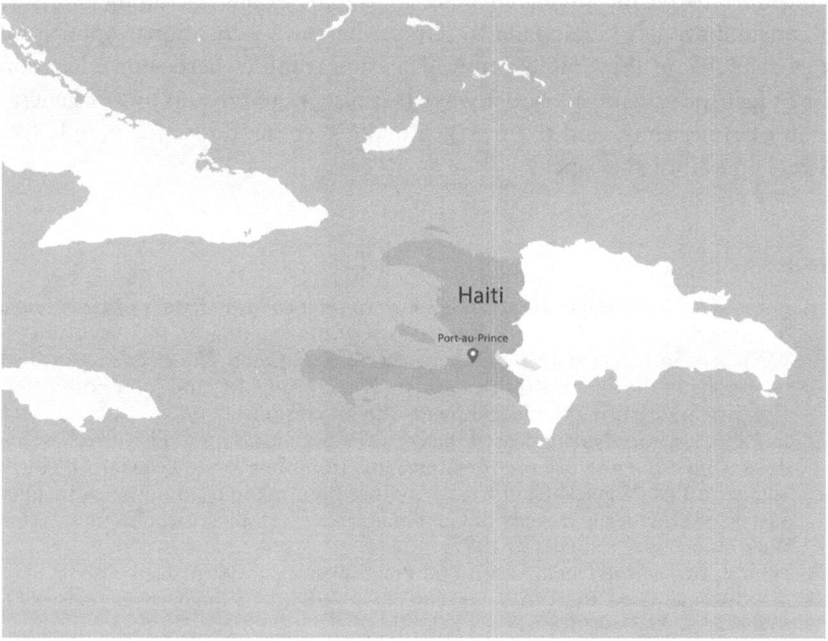

MAP 4.1 Haiti

DISTANCE TO US BORDER: 707 MILES

OBSTACLES TO TRAVEL TO THE UNITED STATES: CARIBBEAN SEA

Source: Captian.N/Shutterstock

4

HAITI

From First Independent Black Republic to Failed State

As we write this chapter, in mid-September 2023, Haiti is living through its most profound sociopolitical crisis in recent history. That's certainly a bold statement for a nation that has experienced political chaos for much of its history—from the time it organized, in the late 18th century, to overthrow its overseas masters, the French.

Tiny Haiti succeeded in overthrowing the West's most significant power at that time—France—and became the first nation in the world to engineer and execute a slave rebellion which led to a democratically structured society. All of this occurred during the time of Thomas Jefferson's presidency (in 1804) and before the Latin American wars of independence.

For its boldness, Haiti has suffered at the hands of the West; the French, after "losing" a profitable sugar-producing colony (which generated, at one point, 40 percent of the French national budget), punished the former colony by insisting on indemnity payments designed to cripple the young Republic. The Americans sided with the French and, in fact, took over the nation for about 20 years starting in 1915. A series of petty dictators were installed by the Americans, most notoriously the "Duvalier" family, which ruled for half the 20th century. A brief skirmish with democracy occurred in the late 20th century when Jean-Bertrand Aristide was elected president in 1990 on a "liberation theology" platform. He was a Roman Catholic priest before engaging in politics.

But even Aristide, who was overthrown by the Haitian military before returning to power with the help of US president Bill Clinton, soon began using harsh, illegal methods against his enemies and was finally sent into exile during his third presidency in 2004.

DOI: 10.4324/9781003357605-5

Fast forward to 2021. On July 7, the sitting president of Haiti was assassinated in his bedroom in the presidential residence. Jovenel Moïse, it appears, had intervened in a profitable drug transportation network that operated in the Caribbean, between Colombia, Central America, and the United States. It seems like he might have asked for a cut (or greater cut) in this lucrative business and was assassinated. Incredibly, the crime has not been officially "solved," though the prime suspect in orchestrating the murder, Rodolphe Jaar, was sentenced in 2023 in a US federal court to life in prison. Much of the planning for the murder happened on US soil, in South Florida.

A malignant stew of international intrigue has characterized this killing. Planned and financed in South Florida, executed by Colombian mercenaries, with the full knowledge of senior military, police, and political figures in Haiti, the crime seems surreal, but points to a tremendous leadership gap in the nation of about 11.5 million.

Now, with the government having literally been "murdered" in 2021, gangs operate with almost absolute impunity, and the social and political situation has gone from bad to worse. Fear of kidnapping has prevented humanitarian aid from entering the nation, and, since the assassination of Moïse, tens of thousands of Haitians have been trying to leave the Caribbean nation that shares a border with an unfriendly and historically hostile neighbor, the Dominican Republic.

It seems as if the West has largely given up on Haiti. President Joe Biden visited Canada in March 2023, and one of the agenda items involved a partnership between the Canadian government and the United States to tackle, together, the political morass in Haiti. Biden returned to Washington with no such agreement in hand.

Nations need friends, and it's sad to note that, historically, Haiti has been roundly condemned and marginalized by world powers like France and the United States for—as noted above—striking out on its own and fighting for independence from its overseas masters. But the Haitians learned a thing or two from their masters and invaded their neighbors to the East (today, the Dominican Republic), occupying the land starting in 1821 for the next 23 years. This adventure was followed by the first Haitian Empire from 1849 to 1859, under Faustin Soulouque. One historian has remarked how Soulouque "was a favorite of Western caricaturists and humorists alike, frequently derided as the black emperor of Haiti who aped European courts."[1] French/Cuban writer and critic Alejo Carpentier captures the madness of this time period in the Caribbean in his classic 1949 novel *The Kingdom of this World.*

Resented by the French and much of the West, ridiculed and feared by its neighbor with which it shares the island known as Hispaniola, Haiti's

19th century was neither progressive nor comparable to its neighbors. The United States, Argentina, and Brazil, for example, were building railroads, encouraging immigration, and building trade networks/export economies that would lead to prosperity in the late 19th century and beyond.

Haiti is unusual in that during the 19th century, many Americans fled the United States and headed to Haiti—in other words, the migratory process we're witnessing today was reversed a century and a half ago. Given that the Haitian revolution—which ended about 1803—effectively eliminated slavery there, many US-enslaved Blacks considered Haiti to be a sort of paradise, and thousands made the voyage there. In 1862, President Lincoln, during the Civil War, supported the migration of some 500 Blacks from the United States to Haiti. Lincoln held a view that was fairly common at the time: While he abhorred slavery, he was somewhat skeptical that Blacks in the United States could be successfully integrated into US society, especially in the South. So, for him, migration to Haiti seemed like an excellent option and opportunity. There was never a sustained or serious migration to Haiti from the United States, though it's likely that some 4,000 to 5,000 made the voyage. Most returned to the United States given the degree of poverty in Haiti, the political instability there, and challenges with the language.

The grimness of the 19th century, and the difficulties imposed on the Haitian people by outside forces and its own limited governments, led to multiple interventions during the 20th century. The United States, after securing the land (by essentially creating the Republic of Panama out of Colombia's territory), built the Panama Canal—which opened in 1914—and passed the "Roosevelt Corollary to the Monroe Doctrine" in 1904. That doctrine is viewed—or was viewed at the time—as a doctrine of intervention. The United States took full advantage of its new authorities/technology in the Caribbean region and, in 1915, intervened in Haiti.

The 20th century, for Haiti, represented a shift away—to some degree—from French affairs as the United States asserted dominance in the region, especially after 1904. The situation for Haiti or the Haitian people didn't necessary improve as a new master essentially stepped in. A brutal massacre of hostages tasked with protecting the new president, Jean Vilbrun Guillaume Sam, led to the public execution of Sam himself; much of the drama occurred in the residence of the French Ambassador, and the American military in 1915 intervened immediately. After 111 years, Haitian independence was no more.

The Americans were concerned with the strategic position of Haiti as it occupied a passageway to and from the Panama Canal via the Windward Passage, "the main sea-lane from New York to the Panama Canal."[2] First World War had begun, and Haiti was too significant—in terms of its geographic locale—to allow for even the remote possibility that it might fall to the Germans. There were improvements made to infrastructure during this time—roads, bridges, schools, and hospitals were built using taxes and fees collected from the Haitian government, but the Americans never completely understood the weight of history, or racism, that defined the Caribbean nation. The American military was still segregated at the time of the occupation, and all of the US officers serving there were white, many from the US South and many openly racist.

The military should have promoted democracy, fair taxation and finance policy, and constitutional governance in Haiti. Yet, in 1938, four years after they left in 1934, the Haitian president, Sténio Vincent, declared a dictatorship and ruled as such. One year earlier, in 1937, the so-called Parsley Massacre occurred on the border between Haiti and the Dominican Republic. Rafael Trujillo, dictator of the neighboring nation, both feared and loathed the Haitian people because of their darker skin which he contrasted to his own "mixed" race heritage. He was a cruel tyrant and a murderous racist. Perhaps 20,000 Haitians were killed in this border massacre, and President Vincent arranged an indemnity payment of $30 per Haitian killed. Rather than distribute the absurd, insulting sum to the families of the dead Haitians, he kept the money paid to him by the Dominican government.

Many were the push factors at this time, but the 1937 massacre, after decades of US occupation, indicated to many that it was time to leave the Caribbean nation. Haitians seeking and receiving Permanent Lawful Resident status in the United States numbered 207 during the decade of the 1930s. During the 1940s, after the Parsley Massacre and when it seemed unlikely that true political reform would materialize, that number jumped to 823. Of course, these were Haitians who had the means to travel, had money to apply for Visas, and most likely had friends or family already living abroad in the United States.

The 1940s and 1950s were marked by political turmoil and chaos in Haiti—a continuation of the prior patterns. Philippe Girard, a historian of the Haitian nation, writes of "six governments [having come and gone] in a six month period."[3] Elections—marked by fraud—were held in 1957, and a new period in Haitian history began: the era of Duvalier. François "Papa Doc" Duvalier was a physician who helped poor marginalized Black Haitians in their quest to achieve better healthcare outcomes. But Duvalier also developed a discourse based on the racism he understood and used to advance his own political gains: lighter-skinned "mulattos" [mixed raced] Haitians discriminated against their Black fellow citizens, most of whom remained at the lower stratum of the socioeconomic pyramid. Duvalier, a dark-skinned man, exploited such thoroughly ingrained national racism to rise to power—with the support of Black or dark-skinned Haitians. He ruled through brutal repression and created his own paramilitary force, the *macoutes*, who were loyal to the regime. One of the reasons Haiti is in such turmoil today is directly related to this paramilitary terror organization, which never really disbanded and today is referred to by the more generic term "gangs." Duvalier is responsible for tens of thousands of deaths—maybe as many as 40,000—during his 31 years of rule as "President for Life."[4]

Where was the United States while all this mayhem and murder occurred in the Caribbean? During the Cold War, which lasted from the conclusion of the Second World War in 1945 until the fall of the Soviet Union (1991), the US policy in the region was strictly focused on "containment" of Communism; thus, any anticommunist leader, as murderous as he might be, received (generally speaking) the support—and more importantly—recognition and military aid from the United States. Really *bad hombres* like Duvalier, Trujillo, Somoza in nearby Nicaragua, Batista on the Caribbean Island of Cuba—and the list goes on—all of these leaders created more instability in their nations due to their undemocratic practices and ruthlessness. The United States looked on with mostly benign indifference, as long as all of the leaders were vociferously anti-Communist.

Naturally, Duvalier's "policies" pushed people out of Haiti—and toward, mostly, the United States. The historic tensions with the neighboring Dominican Republic prevented people from migrating there, so many made the difficult decision to travel to the United States—both legally and otherwise. During the 1960s, 29,000 Haitians arrived in the United States and obtained lawful permanent resident status. During the next decade that number doubled (nearly) to 55,161 and doubled again, during the decade of the 1980s, to 121,406.

Four years after the fall of "Baby Doc" Duvalier, a young Roman Catholic priest steeped in the "theology of liberation"—a theory that emerged in Latin America in the 1960s that challenged the poor to become agents of change in the region and in their own communities—was elected president of Haiti. Jean-Bertrand Aristide's liberationist rhetoric was viewed as "revolutionary" by the military and conservative forces, and he was quicky ousted from power. This military takeover in September 1991 caused a significant exodus from Haiti to the United States, many arriving in rickety boats and other unseaworthy crafts. President Bill Clinton focused on the Haiti situation when he became president in January 1993. Aristide successfully lobbied in the United States, in Congress and with the Congressional Black Caucus. In 1994, after threat of a massive military landing by the United States, the "Generals" relinquished power back to the democratically elected Aristide.

In 2000, Aristide won the presidency again, but was pushed out—this time with the help of the United States—in 2004. A lot had changed from the first coup. First, George W. Bush was president of the United States and had little love for Aristide, his liberationist rhetoric, or the poor people who backed him. Second, in the post-9/11 world, the United States certainly preferred "military" rulers in the region versus former Roman Catholic priests and so, with the help of the US government, Aristide was sent back into exile in 2004. This time he was sent to South Africa via the Central African Republic.

During this decade of turmoil, the 1990s, about 177,000 Haitians left for the United States, many arriving in Miami where they began to establish a community, "Little Haiti," in a rundown northwest segment of the city. Many more arrived, of course, but the 177,000 number reflects the Haitian migrants who were officially and legally recorded. Aristide's removal was followed by a brief incursion by the US Marines who served as a sort of "advance guard" for the tens of thousands of UN troops who arrived on a peacekeeping mission. The mission was led by the Brazilians.

The peacekeeping mission remained in Haiti for 13 years (from 2004 to 2017) and was deemed responsible for an outbreak of cholera that killed about 10,000 Haitian citizens. The outbreak was tied to Nepalese troops stationed in Haiti. Earlier that same year (2010), a massive earthquake leveled Port-au-Prince, killing 200,000 Haitians and displacing about a million. The earthquake really seemed like a cruel seismic curse given the extent of damage and collapse of the National Palace, the French Renaissance-styled residence of the president; "The White House" of Haiti, only much larger. As of this writing, the Palace has not been rebuilt, though it was announced in 2017 by then president Moïse that plans were underway to rebuild. As mentioned earlier in this chapter, Moïse was assassinated in July 2021 in his official residence in Port-au-Prince.

Where to Go?

Obviously, the closest border for Haitians is the one separating their nation from the Dominican Republic, directly East. That border is about 238 miles long and separates, literally, two worlds. Since about 1915, when the Americans invaded, Haitians traveled to the Dominican Republic as a sort of last resort. There they were received grudgingly and came to work in the low-wage agriculture industry (harvesting sugar, mostly) and in construction. The influx of Haitians at the beginning of the 20th century provoked a cruel reaction—discussed above—from Dominican authorities, the so-called Parsley Massacre of 1937. People were rounded up and executed based on their pronunciation of the world parsley in Spanish—*perejil.* A native Spanish speaker could trill or "roll" the "r" in that word; a native Haitian Kreyol speaker could not. This is literally how the Dominican authorities determined who would live and who would die. Maybe 12,000–20,000 people died in this savage, one-week massacre.

There are probably half a million Haitians living in the Dominican Republic, or about 4 percent of the population of that nation. In 2022, there was, once again, a push to deport Haitians after many Haitians arrived at the Dominican border in the wake of the Moïse assassination and the resultant political instability.

The Push Factors

The "push" factors out of Haiti are many, complex and historic. Haitians have been pushed to other parts of Latin America, including Chile and Brazil in recent times and particularly after the 2010 earthquake. A robust economy in Chile provided jobs in the lower end of the spectrum, and Haitians worked in construction, restaurants, and as domestics. But a backlash by the right-of-center Piñera government—Juan Sebastián Piñera—who served as president from 2010 to 2014 and again from 2018 to 2022 developed, especially as the economy, though stable, witnessed a gradual slowdown due to a drop in the price of copper, a significant Chilen export.

In Brazil, Haitians were welcomed as laborers in the construction of the 2014 World Cup and stadiums for the 2016 Olympics. Once these projects were completed, and the reactionary, anti-immigration Jair Bolsonaro arrived at the presidency in 2018, Haitians no longer felt welcome in Brazil, and they left: they traveled from Brazil (and Chile) to the United States.

The United States has always been the preferred destination for Haitians, and currently there are about one million and one hundred thousand Haitians (officially) in the United States, though that number is probably significantly higher.

The Pull Factors

There are a myriad of factors pulling Haitians away from Haiti and toward the United States. First, there is the rhetoric of the United States as a land of unlimited opportunity with clear democratic principles and a commitment to rewarding hard work. The United States—particularly during the era of slavery—didn't always meet those lofty ideals, and in the US South, racial animus and the legacy of slavery have haunted the land and its politics, traditions, and culture. Even when the United States was invading their land with the Marines—and sticking around for nearly two decades—the nation was still seen as aspirational for Haitians, who long ago had given up on their own government or leaders. In the decade following the earthquake (of 2010), about 200,000 Haitians arrived in the United States as lawful permanent residents. Miami's "Little Haiti" was the closest stop for people arriving from Haiti and that neighborhood continues to thrive today as a center of Haitian culture and tradition. People feel comfortable in Miami due to familiarity with language, the mild tropical weather, and the proximity to the homeland. There are other synergies that tie together the Haitian community in South Florida: for example, Miami-Dade College enrolls thousands of Haitian students each year (it's one of the largest community colleges in the nation), and Florida International University offers a Haitian Studies Program (students can earn a certificate in Haitian Studies) and a respected Haitian Summer Institute, where students from all over the world gather to learn about Haitian history and culture while focusing on the Kreyol language.

Earlier in the 20th century, about the time of the Marine Landing (in 1915) Haitians would have fled to New York City—a vibrant, growing, hub of international commerce and technology. It was later in the century, after the Duvalier "election" in 1957, when Miami became an option for Haitians and (soon after) for Cubans, who would flee the excesses of Fidel Castro when he took power in early 1959.

Miami was open, land was plentiful, sunshine was abundant, and public schools were free for the children of immigrants. People began migrating "there" from New York, which by the 1950s and 1960s had become expensive, taxes were high, and crime had taken over many neighborhoods. Haitians first arrived in Harlem in the 1920s and then migrated out to Queens and eventually to Flatbush and other areas of Brooklyn.

Another American city that has attracted a significant number of Haitians is Boston. In areas of Roxbury, Dorchester, and Mattapan, there are significant numbers of Haitians, but Haitian immigrants have been attracted to outlying suburban towns and cities such as Randolph and Brockton. Brockton was once a thriving shoe town, but when that industry collapsed in the 1950s the city fell on hard times. Real estate devalued, and people from the Caribbean—including Haitians—moved in. According to a recent (2021) University of Massachusetts, Boston study, there are about 9,000 foreign-born Haitians living in Brockton, Massachusetts.[5]

US Immigration Law and Haiti

Starting in 1972, Haitians sought protections and the ability to migrate to the United States; this was in response to the Duvalier dictatorship which had grown arbitrary and cruel—more so after having passed into the hands of Jean-Claude "Baby Doc" Duvalier—son of the original dictator, Papa Doc (François). Not until 1980—at the end of the Carter Administration—did the United States change its immigration laws to offer people around the world the right to seek asylum in the United States if they could prove that they had "a well-founded fear of persecution" based on their religious or political activities—the list has been expanded to include people who are members of the LGTBQ community—but it has always excluded "economic" asylum seekers. In other words, people could not arrive in the United States and claim that poverty and an inability to make a decent living at home were primary motivating factors.

The situation grew tense for Haitians precisely in 1980. At the beginning of the "Mariel" boatlift—discussed previously in the chapter on Cuba—the contradiction in US policy could no longer be overlooked. About 125,000 Cubans were admitted to the United States between April and October 1980 as political refugees, people escaping Fidel Castro's Communist Island. Haitians, who had been arriving in the United States and denied access (they were escaping an equally, if not more, repressive government that the United States supported), complained about the absurdity of the policy. They strongly suggested that the policy was motivated by racism (most of the arriving Haitians were Black) and a myopic, one-dimensional understanding of Caribbean politics and society.

Jimmy Carter changed course and allowed in, on a temporary basis, about 25,000 Haitians during this period in 1980. While Cubans were released into the city of Miami to live and thrive with their families (after initial processing), many Haitians were sent to the notorious Krome Detention Center, 15 miles west of Miami in the middle of the Everglades.

When Ronald Reagan became president in January 1981, he decided to continue the old policy—i.e., we would welcome Cubans who arrived at our shores, but would turn Haitians away. A new policy of "Interdiction at Sea" was invoked in 1981; by this policy, United States ships would patrol the Caribbean and prevent people from proceeding toward the United States. The policy was designed to prevent people from making risky journeys—from Haiti, or anywhere else in the Caribbean—to the United States. From 1981 to 1991 some 25,000 Haitians were returned to their home. Only 28 were allowed to seek protection under the US legal system.[6]

For Haiti, 1991 was a critical year. First, democratic elections were held for the first time in the nation's history. Jean-Bertrand Aristide was elected, but by September of the same year he was pushed out of the presidency in a military coup. Thousands of people took to creaky, dangerous crafts to make the trip to the United States; thousands perished at sea. Many were allowed to pursue asylum claims but most were returned (by the George H.W. Bush Administration) to Haiti. Neither the United States nor any nation of Latin America was prepared to help the Haitian people during this period of political, economic, and social crisis. The problem, like today, seemed intractable, and the West has been largely reluctant to help poor, dark-skinned Haitians. This has been a tragic historic constant since about 1804.

The tragedy of Aristide involves the word "hope." The international community—particularly the young, dynamic Clinton Administration in

Washington (1993–2000) worked energetically and creatively to support Aristide. Clinton organized a military flotilla designed to push Aristide back into power in 1994, and the Haitian military that had deposed Aristide relented at the last moment, and the elected president returned to power and served until 1996. He was elected again in 2000 and ousted in a military coup in early 2004. Aristide has claimed that he was essentially kidnapped by the US government, which provided a 757 jet to carry him out of the country. He was taken to the Central African Republic and eventually settled into exile in South Africa.

By 2004, the US government, firmly under control of Republican George W. Bush, viewed Aristide as a destabilizing element for Haitian society. In 2004, the United States provided about $3 million in humanitarian aid to Haiti, but that amount would hardly solve the socioeconomic problems of Haiti and would soon be overshadowed by the billions of dollars that would flow into the nation after the devastating earthquake of 2010. That earthquake literally demolished the capital city of Port-au-Prince.

2010: The Earthquake and Some New Policies

The 2010 earthquake resulted in some 200,000 deaths and the destruction of the National Palace. It also generated about $13.5 billion in aid from foreign governments and entities and a visit from "The Sunshine Boys" (Former Presidents Bill Clinton and George W. Bush, working the rope line together) and Sean Penn. Much of the money disappeared; it certainly didn't help to create a stable, democratic, or economically viable nation. This earthquake, together with a subsequent cholera outbreak—brought to the nation by Nepalese Peacekeepers assigned to Haiti under a UN mandate—created yet another wave of out-migration from Haiti.

TPS—Temporary Protective Status—was announced by then Homeland Security director Janet Napoletano in the immediate aftermath of the January 2010 earthquake. TPS is a form of temporary relief from deportation proceedings and is designated for nations that are undergoing a war or some sort of environmental disaster (think Hurricane Mitch in Honduras, 1998) which prevents people living in the United States without documentation from returning home and seeking secure work or a stable political environment. The grant of TPS was originally applied for 18 months, subject to review and renewal by the Secretary, and at the time (in 2010) was believed to affect about 200,000 Haitians living without documentation in the United States. Haitians living in the United States (prior to the earthquake) could file a form with the Department of Homeland Security, pay a filing fee, and demonstrate a clean criminal record. Once those and other conditions were met, Haitians living in the United States would not be deported. In January 2023, TPS was once again extended, through August 2024.

So, TPS has been one policy option for Haitians living in the United States; other countries, too, have received this designation, or protection, including Honduras, El Salvador, and Nicaragua (in Latin America), and Nepal and Sudan in other corners of the world. TPS protections, it should be remembered, apply to people already living in the United States.

After the earthquake, the next crisis, political, came in 2015/16 with elections largely seen as compromised given that the 2015 scheduled elections had been "scrapped." Irregularities in the schedules of elections, cancellations of elections, and other concerns were resolved when Jovenel Moïse won the presidential election in late 2016 with about 600,000 votes, but the opponents cried foul, resulting in widespread protests. Eventually, in February 2017, Moïse was seated as the president of the republic. By early 2018, the congress and executive were at odds as to term lengths, election schedules, and basic "housekeeping" details concerning the democratic process.

Next, in July 2021, as mentioned above, President Moïse was assassinated by a crew of 26 Colombian mercenaries and two Haitian-Americans; a few of the Colombians had received training in US military academies. The president's political enemies were seen as responsible for the crime, one of whom is serving a life sentence in a US federal prison after being convicted of plotting the execution, Mr. Rodolphe Jaar (a Haitian-Chilean businessman). Others are heading to trial as we prepare this text, but a strange stew of businesspeople, politicians, and military—all of whom wanted the president killed—are seen as responsible for Moïse's assassination.

The assassination, on July 7, 2021, was followed by a major earthquake in August in the Haitian countryside. Since then, the nation has descended into chaos, with gangs in control of at least 60 percent of the capital city, Port-au-Prince. This latest, mostly man-made crisis has sparked yet another round of emigration out of Haiti, and in 2023 the Biden Administration offered Haitians "Parole" status. Thousands of Haitians who had once been living in Chile, Brazil, and other places in Latin America decided to try and gain entrance into the United States; they were discouraged from returning home to Haiti, particularly after the events of 2021.

On October 2, 2023, a new UN international security mission was agreed to. Led by Kenya, the mission will deploy a force of 2,500; about 200 Kenyan police arrived in Haiti in June 2024 to prepare for the security initiative. The force hopes to neutralize armed gangs that control most of the capital city. Sixty million dollars was pledged in humanitarian aid by US Ambassador to the United Nations, Linda Thomas-Greenfield in a July 2024 visit to the

Caribbean nation. It has taken more than three years for the international community to acknowledge the extent of the catastrophic situation in Haiti and hopefully the Kenyan forces will be more successful than the previous UN mission, led by Brazil, which most acknowledge was a failure. The Brazilian led mission lasted for 13 years, from 2004 to 2017. During that period, the elected president (Aristide) was ousted, a major earthquake destroyed the capital city, and shortly thereafter a cholera epidemic (originating with the Peacekeepers) led to about 10,000 Haitian deaths.

A recent policy initiative that has affected Haitian migrants involves the so-called Title 42. Title 42 is (or was) a somewhat obscure ruling on public health that allowed the US government to turn away immigrants to our shores during a public health emergency. COVID-19 represented just such an emergency, and Title 42 restrictions were enforced in the United States from 2020 to 2023. The United States expelled 2.8 million people seeing asylum during this dire period in our history. Title 42 was finally lifted during the Biden Administration: the ruling expired on May 11, 2023, and had been enforced since pandemic restrictions began in March 2020.

In 2023, Haitians (together with Cubans, Nicaraguans, and Venezuelans) were offered a "Parole" protection assuming they could arrive in the United States; they would have to arrive in the United States in a lawful manner (i.e., at an approved point of entry) and have "sponsorship" in the United States. Such sponsorship could be any US citizen offering protection, housing, and material support during a two-year period. Each month 30,000 "Paroles" are being offered in an attempt to calm the intense pressures at the US southern borders. Also, each country mentioned above has seen its share of political upheaval recently. From the assassination of the sitting president (Haiti, July 2021), to the collapse of the Venezuelan economy and oil industry under President Maduro, to the arbitrary, erratic rule of Daniel Ortega and his wife (who ran as Ortega's vice president during the 2016 elections and is said to essentially run the nation), to the limited democratic structures in place in Cuba—the nations were chosen for their political peculiarities and proximity to the United States. Also, the US government has serious "policy" concerns with each nation, and the less-than-enlightened leadership in each place. In the case of Haiti, there is virtually no functioning government as we write this, in the fall of 2023.

Jean Girard is a 34-year-old who was born in Port-de-Paix in the Northwest section of Haiti; he arrived here in the United States via Canada in May 2023, taking advantage of the Parole system/policy discussed directly above. According to Mr. Girard, "it's easier for Haitians to arrive to the USA, which is more open than Canada" (at the time of our interview in November 2023). Canada, particularly the French-speaking Eastern Province of Quebec, has long held "destination" status for Haitians, given the language familiarity of this democratic, industrialized nation in the Americas. There are perhaps 165,000 Haitians in Canada, the majority living in and around the city of Montreal.

Jean told us that "there is zero cost" associated with Parole in the United States; he merely needed to find a sponsor who would "take him in." Jean is currently waiting for employment authorization which takes a few months—and varies from state to state. He was offered a position as an English as a Second Language (ESL) Interventionist at a local public school in Indiana but can only accept the position after obtaining official authorization to work.

Jean met his wife in Haiti seven years ago, and they're together here in the United States. In May 2023, she graduated from Indiana University with a degree in Public Health Science, having begun the program in August 2018. Nadine, Jean's wife, is trying to change her I–20 student visa but for now, with gangs ruling much of the capital city, returning to Haiti is not an option for the young couple.

Tens of thousands of Haitians have arrived at the US southern border since July 2021—since the assassination of the sitting president; that crime has not been conclusively settled, as of this writing. Sending in 1,000 or 1,500 armed Kenyan Peacekeepers under a UN mandate does not seem to offer many solutions to the Caribbean nation, especially for those of us who remember the last UN mission. The cycle of bad politics, outside intervention, otherworldly corruption, and bad luck in terms of natural catastrophes seems to have condemned Haiti to centuries of despair. But yet over and over again, the Haitian people have proved their resilience against the odds imposed by humankind and the natural environment. It's critically important that the world understands Haitian history and offers to step in from time to time with helpful measures and a welcoming embrace of the Haitian people when they're forced to flee from their homeland.

Notes

1 Philipe Girard, *Haiti.* (New York: Palgrave), 2010, p. 73.
2 Philipe Girard, *Haiti.* (New York: Palgrave), 2010, p. 83.
3 Philipe Girard, *Haiti.* (New York: Palgrave), 2010, p. 97.
4 In 1971, Duvalier died and turned the presidency—again, for life—over to his only son, Jean-Claude. Claude "Baby Doc" Duvalier ruled until he was overthrown in 1986.
5 Phillip Granberry and Vishakha Agarwal, "Latinos in Massachusetts: Brockton." Gastón Institute Publications, 2021. University of Massachusetts at Boston.
6 See a perceptive paper by Patrick Gavigan, "Migration Emergencies and Human Rights in Haiti," 1997. Paper, Conference on Regional Responses to Forced Migration in Central America and the Caribbean.

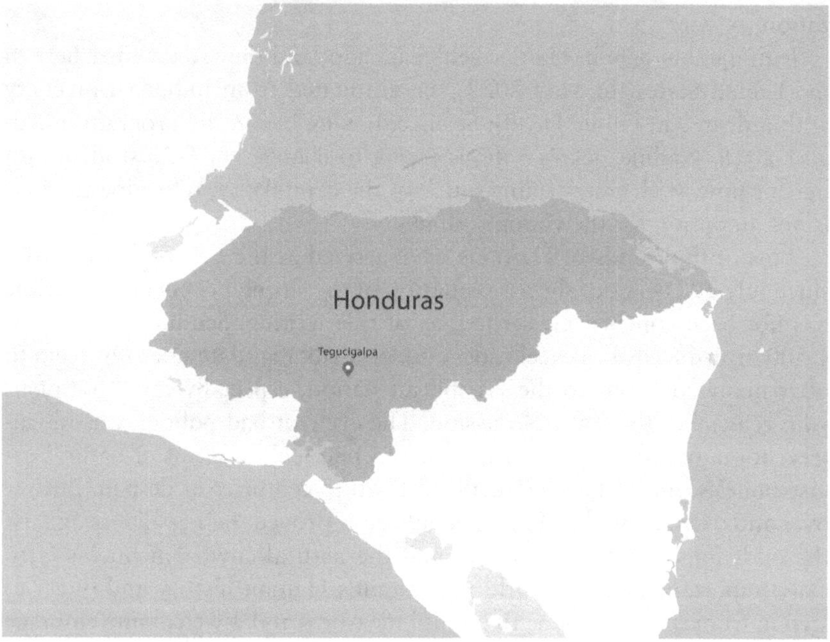

MAP 5.1 Honduras

DISTANCE TO US BORDER: 1,050 MILES

OBSTACLES TO TRAVEL TO THE UNITED STATES: GUATEMALA, MEXICO

Source: Captian.N/Shutterstock

5

HONDURAS

A Quarter Century Post-Mitch

Sitting in the center of Central America, Honduras occupies little space in the minds or imagination of most Americans. Most probably, they associate the country with the large numbers of *catrachos*, the nickname for Hondurans, who have braved thousands of dangerous miles to attempt to enter through the US southern border. Some know of the gang violence on Honduran streets or the historically high murder rates. Or some recognize the country's name from the tags on their clothes or the stickers on their fruit. Despite its rich history and deep ties to the United States, Honduras remains largely a mystery to most Americans.

About 43,000 square miles, or roughly the size of the state of Ohio, Honduras is home to an array of ecosystems packed inside its borders. The central and southwest portions of the country are marked by mountain ranges with oak-pine forests giving way to the humidity and moisture of cloud forests at higher altitudes. These cloud forests, like La Tigra or Celaque National Parks, are unique moisture-rich environments full of epiphytes—plants or organisms that grow on the surface of other plants—and contain abundant wildlife including the Resplendent Quetzal and the Golden-cheeked Warbler.

The northern coast extending east into the Río Plátano Biosphere Reserve, a UNESCO World Heritage site, is a mixture of dense rainforest, broadleaf forests, mangroves, and marshes. These lands are home to the majority of the nearly 800 species of birds that reside in the country. The far eastern department of Gracias a Dios, which is largely cut off from the rest of the country except by plane and boat, contains broad savannas, marshes, and swamps.

DOI: 10.4324/9781003357605-6

Off the northern coast sits the Bay Islands of Roatan, Utila, and Guanaja, within whose clear waters sit some of the most pristine coral reefs in the Caribbean.

Compared to its neighbors, Honduras has relatively little arable land. The fruit companies claimed most of that land in the late 19th and early 20th centuries. Cuyamel Fruit Company, owned by Samuel Zemurray,[1] occupied most of the desirable land in the northwestern portion of the country including much of the land around the Cuyamel River and Puerto Cortes. The Italian-American Vaccaro Brothers occupied the area near La Ceiba, and United Fruit had the land to the east near Trujillo.

The interactions of these three companies guided the history and policy of Honduras in the early 20th century. For example, after the election of Miguel Dávila to the presidency in 1907, the Vaccaro Brothers gained an ally in government who quickly entered into a series of agreements in which the Vaccaro Brothers obtained land grants in exchange for handling the construction of railways, roads, and harbors funded by the Honduran government that would ultimately benefit the Brothers. Zemurray, never one to stand idly by in competition, organized and funded a coup that ultimately led Manuel Bonilla to the presidency. Bonilla, indebted to Zemurray, entered into various agreements with Cuyamel to expand its interests and gain funding and land rights for the development of its own infrastructure.

Cuyamel and Zemurray's aggressive expansion nearly led to a war in 1915 as Cuyamel began to move production into the Motagua Valley along the border with Guatemala and attempted to build a railroad across the disputed border. Guatemala—funded and supported by United Fruit—defended against the incursion. A US-led mediation avoided a full-scale conflict.

Between 1911 and 1929, the United States intervened six times to defend and maintain the interests of the fruit companies in Honduras. In 1929, Cuyamel and United Fruit merged and consolidated interests, which largely resolved two decades of conflicts.

The fruit companies' occupation of much of the northern coast of Honduras opened up the earliest waves of immigration to the United States from Honduras. All three companies largely used New Orleans as their primary port for banana imports. Early enclaves of Hondurans first called New Orleans home in the 1910s as ships brought bananas and workers across the Caribbean and the Gulf of Mexico.

The number of Hondurans in New Orleans continued to grow and by the 1950s and 1960s, a community of Hondurans coalesced in the Lower Garden District, which they referred to as *El Barrio Lempira*, which was named after the Lenca leader and warrior who briefly fought the Spanish conquest and inspired other native indigenous groups to resist the Spanish. Even by 1970, the largest community of Hondurans in the United States was still less than 10,000.[2]

Despite the banana companies occupying large swaths of the richest land for agriculture, Honduras initially avoided the conflicts over land reform and the seemingly inevitable civil wars that followed in their neighboring countries. Between 1962 and 1980, aided by a confluence of well-organized workers from the banana plantations, sympathetic public officials, and Hurricane Fifi's destruction of plantations held by the fruit companies in 1974, nearly a quarter of landless families obtained land. In the wake of the hurricane, the banana companies donated what for the companies had become useless land. Much of this land was held and worked through cooperatives or *cooperativas* in the Bajo Aguán Valley. During the near 20-year land reform effort, landless Hondurans also benefited from the expulsion of between 60,000 and 130,000 Salvadorans, many of whom occupied unclaimed land in Honduras, after the 1969 Football War.[3]

Those land reform efforts contributed to relatively few Hondurans leaving for the United States. Indeed, by 1980, only around 40,000 Hondurans called the United States home.

The period of significant land reform in the mid- to late 1970s coincided with the growth of the *maquila* movement in Honduras. Maquiladoras or maquilas are manufacturing or assembly facilities that operate in established duty-free or tariff-free zones. Typically, a country in the economically developing world, like Honduras, will establish a zone in which businesses, often from the United States, Europe, or Asia, can assemble or manufacture their finished products without being taxed on the importation of the raw materials. The theory is that companies get a cheap source of labor and the host country obtains jobs for its citizens. In 1976, Honduras established its first duty-free zone in Puerto Cortes, located in the northeast of country along the Bahía de Omoa.

Over the next ten years, upheaval in neighboring El Salvador, Guatemala, and Nicaragua sent significant numbers of refugees, asylum seekers, and migrants north to the United States. The number of Hondurans in the United States in that period more than doubled to approximately 100,000, but remained below that of its neighbors whose populations in the United States had expanded significantly (Nicaragua—164,000; Guatemala—213,000; El Salvador—459,000).

During this same period, the United States spent millions of dollars training and arming the military and anti-communist rebels in El Salvador and Nicaragua, largely from within Honduras. Nevertheless, Honduras escaped much of the violence that plagued the rest of Central America in the 1980s.

Hurricane Mitch and the Start of an Exodus

The most significant waves of immigration to the United States from Honduras did not begin until the late 1990s. The single largest catalyst, which initiated a nearly 30-year exodus, was Hurricane Mitch. Mitch upended the politics, economy, environment, and security of the country. It also exposed the tenuousness with which most of Honduran society lived on a daily basis.

Hurricane Mitch formed into a hurricane on October 25, 1998, and then quickly developed into a Category 5 storm with winds of 180 mph. Off the coast of Honduras, the storm slowed and was downgraded to a Category 1 hurricane by the time it made landfall in Honduras on October 29, 1998. Despite winds dropping to 80 mph at landfall, Hurricane Mitch brought a tremendous amount of precipitation in the form of between one and two feet per day of rain. Mitch sat over the country dumping torrents of rain, which caused unprecedented flooding, mudslides, and damage to infrastructure. By the time it left Honduras on October 31, 1998, between 7,000 and 15,000 people had died, up to 1.5 million were homeless, and the country's infrastructure and potable water systems suffered critical damage. The then Honduran president Carlos Flores estimated that Mitch set economic development back by 50 years.

In the wake of this disaster, the attorney general of the United States on January 5, 1999, under section 244 of the Immigration and Nationality Act, designated Hondurans present in the United States from December 30, 1998, the Temporary Protected Status, or TPS. TPS is a program passed by Congress in 1990, partially as a result of the civil war in El Salvador, that allows individuals present in the United States to be granted temporary protected status in the United States when the conditions of their home country are deemed to be unsafe because of natural disasters, protected unrest, or conflict. TPS designation only confers protection from deportation, employment eligibility, and travel authorization for up to 18 months unless renewed by the Secretary of Homeland Security. The TPS designation may be renewed repeatedly and indefinitely based on the conditions of the home country. Critically, temporary protected status is just that—temporary. It does not confer or create a pathway to permanent residency or citizenship.

Approximately 86,000 Hondurans were recipients of TPS, which created a legal category for normalization, no matter how tenuous and temporary, of Hondurans' immigration status in the United States.

For most, like Ana Madero, TPS provided a previously unknown level of stability. Ana had immigrated to the United States in 1996 after she and her then partner faced extortion and threats from a group of men who were involved in organized crime. She crossed the border between Mexico and the United States without inspection and landed in Memphis, Tennessee. She worked two full-time jobs with only four hours rest between them as she scrapped to pay for her life in the United States. Ana sent most of her earnings back to Honduras, where she had been forced to leave her four children.

In 1999, after Hurricane Mitch, Ana became eligible for TPS. This change in status allowed her to secure more stable, higher-paying work. She established roots, married, and obtained residency through her citizen husband.

After 25 years, approximately 56,000 Hondurans still have TPS. Honduras, which escaped the civil and anti-communist wars and genocides of its neighbors in the 1970s–1980s, did not benefit from the immigration relief that was granted to individuals from those Central American and Caribbean countries. For example, the Nicaraguan Adjustment and Central American Relief Act (NACARA), passed in 1997, created a path to residency for hundreds of thousands of Salvadoran, Guatemalan, Nicaraguan, and Cuban nationals who fled their home countries. Even before NACARA, the small number of Hondurans in the United States in the 1980s when the United States passed the Immigration Reform and Control Act of 1986 also meant that Hondurans did not benefit significantly from the "Reagan amnesty."

As a result, the future flow of immigrants from Honduras to the United States would have few avenues for regularization of their immigration status as TPS provides only temporary protection and no ability to petition for family members once that relief is granted. Further, few Hondurans had family in the United States with whom they could pursue family reunification as a means to gain a recognized immigrant status.

Despite those few avenues for legal immigration to the United States available to Hondurans, the 25 years post-Mitch would show a dramatic increase in immigration from Honduras to the United States. The Pew Hispanic Trust estimates that the Honduran population in the United States grew from 2000 to 2021 from 180,000 to 700,000, a growth of 284 percent.[4] The total population of those with a Honduran origin in the United States (foreign-born plus US-born to Honduran parents) jumped 374 percent during that same period, reaching a total population of 1.1 million.[5]

Four factors—a lack of economic opportunity, high crime, an ineffective/corrupt government, and an increase in environmental disasters as a result of climate change—acting in concert have driven citizens from Honduras in historic numbers to the United States with the highest concentrations in Texas, Florida, California, New York, and North Carolina.

Bajo Aguán Valley[6]

In 1992, despite the success of the previous 20 years of land reform, Honduras passed a law permitting the sale of huge swaths of land to private corporations that previously could only be held collectively. Large-scale agro-industrial groups quickly descended and gobbled up thousands of acres. Dinant Corporation, and its expanding palm oil production, has led these advances. Campesinos and campesino organizations have challenged the validity of many of those sales and sought to overturn the possession of that property through administrative and court action.

These efforts to resolve conflicts through governmental challenges, however, have done little to quell the unrest in the region. In fact, private security companies, perhaps more accurately characterized as paramilitary groups, killed more than 100 campesino activists between 2009 and 2014. A Human Rights Watch investigation of 29 of those killings found the local Honduran authorities, both police and prosecutors, to be completely ineffective in preventing, investigating, and prosecuting these crimes.

This spate of killings came on the heels of the 2009 coup of President Manuel Zelaya Rosales. Zelaya, at the time a member of the Liberal Party, was elected in 2006 following the four-year term of Ricardo Maduro. Maduro, a National Party candidate, followed a tough-on crime approach and placed the military with machine guns on the street alongside local police in an effort to address crime and the growing gang problem.

Zelaya promised a very different presidency, one focused on addressing poverty and systemic educational deficiencies. Upon taking office, Zelaya increased the minimum wage, reduced interest rates, and introduced a series of educational reforms. The increase in minimum wage was wildly popular in Honduras. During his presidency, Zelaya continued to move left in his political calculations signing an agreement to join the Venezuelan-led Bolivarian Alternative for the Americas (ALBA). This effort led to growing concern in conservative circles in Washington and in Honduras, especially in the military.

With an election coming in 2009, Zelaya began to push the idea of seeking a constitutional assembly to rewrite the Honduran constitution. Zelaya then announced that Hondurans would vote in the June 2009 ballot on the question of whether a constitutional assembly to rewrite the constitution should be placed on the November 2009 ballot. Zelaya saw this as a step to demonstrate that the people of Honduras were behind his plans for reform. Conservatives in Honduras and outside the country believed—or at least justified their subsequent actions by claiming they believed—that Zelaya was seeking to redraw the constitution in order to eliminate any term limits and keep himself in power, just as Hugo Chávez had done in Venezuela.

On June 28, 2009, after having refused to distribute the June ballots, the Honduran military forcefully removed Zelaya at gunpoint in his pajamas from the presidential palace, placed him on a private plane, and flew him to Costa Rica. Roberto Micheletti, president of the Honduran congress and National Party member, then declared himself president.

A report by *The Intercept* found considerable links between the military perpetrators of the coup and the US. military both before and after

Zelaya's removal from the country. It was perhaps more than ironic that the Honduran military's transfer of President Zelaya from one plane to another that ultimately flew him to Costa Rica took place on the runway of Soto Cano, the US military air base in Honduras.

While President Obama decried the actions as a coup initially, the State Department led by Hillary Clinton sent mixed messages. Its negotiations—both direct and through the OAS—dragged on, and ultimately the perpetrators of the coup were able to ride out the rest of President Zelaya's term. The National Party won the next election—a contest boycotted by Zelaya and his party—and would rule until 2022.

With the installation of a right-wing government in 2009, the effort of the Zelaya administration to broker a resolution to the growing conflict for the *campesinos* of Bajo Aguán disappeared. The local police, prosecutors, and state prosecutors have shown themselves to be either incompetent, disinterested, underresourced, or simply unwilling to investigate and prosecute the perpetrators of these crimes. What had been a regional example of successful land reform had become a war zone.

The 2008 Recession, a Coup, a Pandemic, Environmental Disaster, and Violent Crime

The 2009 coup could not have hit Honduras at a worse time. The country was still reeling from the effects of the 2008 global recession, and the civil unrest resulting from the coup struck a major blow to societal stability. In 2009, Honduras suffered a 3 percent drop in the GDP, fiscal revenues fell 13 percent, and revenue from foreign trade dropped by 25 percent.[7]

Shortly thereafter, the new right-wing governments that followed Zelaya began to undo the social safety nets that he had created. These governments created carve-outs from minimum wage and labor protections by creating new classes of exempt workers and limited the government's ability to tax and oversee foreign investment under the guise of a free market. The poverty rate, which had been dropping precipitously over the previous five years, rose dramatically.

The *maquila* industry in Honduras had grown at a very high rate in the years preceding the coup. In 2007, the industry in Honduras grew at a rate of 32.7 percent and 11.6 percent in 2008.[8] The maquila sector stagnated in 2009, growing only 2.9 percent.[9]

While the percentage of the population in extreme poverty continually, though moderately dropped between 2012 and 2019, the COVID-19 pandemic inflicted severe economic suffering on the people of Honduras. In 2019, 59.3 percent of Hondurans were living in poverty.[10] By July 2021, the poverty rate by one estimate had jumped to 73.6 percent.[11]

In March 2020, the Honduran government placed its people under strict lockdown restrictions that exacerbated the existing strains on its poorest citizens. In August 2020, a World Food Program and International Organization for Migration survey found that 68 percent of those who responded expressed concern over having enough food to eat.

In concert with the economic downturns and the quarantine restrictions, the Honduran government failed to provide the type of social safety net support that kept the US economy afloat during the early portion of the pandemic. Instead, due to widespread corruption, the Honduran government passed legislative packages that spent millions in aid while producing few deliverables.

As Hondurans struggled to survive the stressors of the pandemic, they were caught with brutal back-to-back punches in the form of successive category 4 hurricanes that struck the country within two weeks. Hurricane Eta hit Honduras on November 6, 2020, and was followed 12 days later by Hurricane Iota. Collectively these storms caused approximately $2 billion in damages accounting for approximately 8 percent of Honduras's GDP.[12] While not resulting in nearly as many deaths as Hurricane Mitch, these storms did comparable damage to the agricultural sector as well as infrastructure, displacing more than 350,000 people.[13]

The Honduran government learned few lessons from Hurricane Mitch and was caught unprepared as the then president Juan Orlando Hernández's government ignored repeated warnings of the incoming disaster in favor of preparation for a national holiday promoting tourism. As the Migration Policy Institute succinctly noted:

> even if the government had been prompt in its response, it was not prepared to handle the crisis. The recently appointed head of COPECO [the Honduran agency tasked with responding to such disasters], a former reggaeton star named Max Alejandro Gonzáles Bonilla (who went by the stage name Killa), admitted he had no experience managing disasters and was unqualified for the job.[14]

While the Honduran economy has suffered from corruption, crime, environmental disasters, and a pandemic, remittances from the United States have grown at a concerningly high rate. In 1998, when Hurricane Mitch struck Honduras, remittances constituted approximately 3.5 percent of the national GDP.[15] In 2022, remittances constituted more than 25 percent of the Honduran GDP.[16]

Indeed, the story of Manuel Vallejo is particularly illustrative of the problems posed by the Honduran economy and how it drives migrants to the United States. Manuel is from San Francisco de Soroguara, a picturesque town of 900 people in the mountains approximately 45 minutes from the nation's capital, Tegucigalpa. According to Manuel, nearly every family in Soroguara has someone his age living and working in the United States and sending back money to their families. Manuel, who graduated with a *bachelerato* in business, was unable to find work in his field. He worked in the maquila zone in the Amarateca Valley and then in a toll booth. Neither of these positions provided Manuel with the security and satisfaction he desired. He ultimately felt that he had no choice but to travel to the United States, a journey that took nearly 30 days.

Manuel never wanted to leave his hometown and finds little enjoyment in life in the United States, where he is working 12-hour days for a residential and commercial roofing company. He is saving money and sending payments back to his family with the hope that within a year or two he can return to his life and family in San Francisco. "Life is expensive here. Everything costs money. In Soroguara, it's more relaxed."

In Honduras, perhaps no greater push factor for emigration exists than crime. Honduras is routinely rated as one of the most violent countries in the Western Hemisphere. The roots of violent crime in Honduras, like most of Central America, reside in the Los Angeles of the 1980s, where Central Americans, especially Salvadorans, landed as they sought refuge from a brutal civil war.

Central Americans, largely residing in the poorest part of Los Angeles, found themselves the target of street gangs and were excluded from membership in the existing Mexican gangs at the time. Out of this combination of poverty, exclusion, and criminal targeting, gangs like Mara Salvatrucha (MS-13) and the 18th Street Gang (Barrio 18) formed and flourished among the Central American population.

Hondurans in those gangs were largely undocumented immigrants who had no legal immigration status to protect them from deportation when arrested. The crackdown began in 1992 with the "Rodney King" riots in Los Angeles. Essentially, the United States sowed the seeds of organized, violent crime and then transplanted it back to the two largest cities in Honduras, San Pedro Sula and Tegucigalpa.

The Honduran murder rate jumped from 10 per 100,000 people in 1990 to a high of 82 per 100,000 in 2011.[17] While the rate had been steadily climbing in the years preceding the 2009 coup, the years of instability that followed did nothing to alleviate the violence on Honduran streets. The murder rate has fallen in the last decade but seemingly leveled out at a still precariously high rate at approximately 40 murders per 100,000 people.[18] By contrast, the US rate is 5.5 per 100,000.

The gangs responsible for this violence have recruited young children and forced them through violence and extortion into their ranks. Faced with this daily threat, many children chose to flee their homes for the United States.

Dorian Wilde is one such child. In 2005, Dorian was just seven years old and followed his mother, who had left five years earlier, to the United States because he was being targeted by gangs on the streets of Tegucigalpa. He sought refuge in the United States but was not eligible for asylum; the narrow definition of who qualifies for such relief forced him and many like him to seek entry without inspection.

Specifically, US law allows individuals to obtain asylum if they can demonstrate that they have been persecuted or have a well-founded fear of persecution because of their race, religion, nationality, membership in a "particular social group," or political opinion. The "particular social group" must be (1) composed of members who share a common immutable characteristic, (2) defined with particularity, and (3) perceived or recognized as a group by society. The attorney general and the courts have failed to establish a consistent interpretation of this standard—with the Trump Administration adopting a rigid application that left most applicants without an avenue for relief and with the Biden Administration attempting to expand the standard. Congressional inaction on the issue for the past 25 years has provided no clarity on US policy nor any relief for those suffering from the gang violence in their home countries that originated on American streets.

As a result, some 14,000 Hondurans, like Dorian, who entered the United States before their 16th birthday and were in the United States continuously for the five years prior to June 15, 2012, have had to rely on Deferred Action for Childhood Arrivals (DACA) to provide some immigration relief.[19] President Obama's executive action created this program that has allowed these young people the opportunity to work and study in the United States with some element of protection from deportation. The future of this program, however, sits in a uncertain legal posture as litigation continues over its propriety.

In addition to children being targeted by gangs for recruitment, women and girls have a precarious and dangerous place in Honduran society. The Economic Commission for Latin America and the Caribbean reported that in 2022 Honduras reported the highest rate of femicide (i.e., the killing of a woman or girl on account of her gender) in Latin America—at 6.0 per 100,000 women, more than twice as high as the nearest country.[20] Put more concretely, for the first ten months of 2023, Statista Research found a total of 341 women were murdered on account of their gender in Honduras.[21]

The local and national governments of Honduras have proven unable or unwilling to combat the issue of crime. According to the Alliance for Peace and Justice 2019, less than a quarter of all homicides in Honduras were even investigated, only 13 percent of all homicides resulted in a conviction, and courts face a backlog of over 180,000 cases.[22] For femicides, UN Women estimates that the conviction rate is even lower, with 90 percent of such crimes going unpunished.[23] In light of these numbers, Hondurans can be left with no conclusion other than that crime is committed with impunity.

While gang recruitment and crime pushed so many citizens north, former Honduran president Juan Orlando Hernández was leading and profiting from a drug-trafficking conspiracy of hundreds of thousands of pounds of cocaine to the United States. Specifically, Hernández, who was extradited to the United States in 2022 after leaving office, was convicted in 2024 of conspiring to import cocaine into the United States with the Sinaloa Cartel and accepting millions of dollars in money, which he then used for his own personal gain and political advantage.

Hernández was not alone among governmental officials in profiting from the drug trade. Honduras's top cop, Five-Star General Juan Carlos Bonilla, who the United States ironically relied upon to assist its efforts to stop drug trafficking from South America, pled guilty to drug trafficking in federal court in early 2024. The United States worked with Bonilla despite his well-known history of human rights abuses such as state-sponsored killings and disappearances.

In light of this violence and corruption, Hondurans looked to new leadership while at the same time turning back the clock to 2009 with the election of Xiomara Castro. Castro, the wife of former president Manuel Zelaya, became in November 2021 the first woman elected president of Honduras. Castro has largely shifted the governmental policies to the left, intervening on behalf of the Lenca indigenous community in a land dispute, banning open-pit mining, and cutting ties with Taiwan in favor of China.

Despite adopting mostly far-left governing policies, Castro, when confronted with the question of crime and violence, looked to Honduras's neighbor, El Salvador, for answers and mimicked Nayib Bukele's ironfisted policing policies. On December 6, 2022, Castro issued Executive Decree Number PCM 20–2022, which suspended six constitutional rights including freedoms of assembly and movement and the rights against warrantless searches and seizures.

The majority of Hondurans largely welcomed Castro's efforts, but the Bukele-esque policy of imprisoning thousands of citizens with little due process has not proven as successful as it was in El Salvador in reducing crime. The murder rate has dropped, but gangs have continued to plague the larger cities, and extortion, violence, and targeted killings of environmentalists and civil activists continue.

Significantly, these policies appear, at least in the last year, to have done little to stem the flow of immigrants to the United States from Honduras. In 2023, the Migrant Policy Institute calculated 214,000 crossings in fiscal year 2023 with Hondurans at ports of entry to the United States.[24] In 2022 at the Southern Border, that number was just over 213,000.[25]

Given the inconsistency in the application of asylum law to those fleeing gang violence and the lack of historical immigration relief targeting Hondurans, much of the immigration to the United States consists of unauthorized immigration and illegal border crossings.

While Honduras has more than 100 years of deep ties to the United States, significant immigration from Honduras to the United States did not begin until the very late 20th century. For the two decades that followed, failed US policy, persistent domestic corruption, high levels of violent crime, repeated environmental disasters, and a weak economy have created the conditions for significant migration to the United States that shows no real signs of abating. Indeed, the critical role that remittances play in the Honduran economy likely guarantees the need for continued immigration to the United States from Honduras unless the domestic economy of Honduras can provide an alternative. No immigration framework or significant pathways for legal migration presently exist that would allow any substantial number of Hondurans to legally cross into the United States. In light of these conditions, Hondurans will continue to seek refuge in a place where they believe they and their families will have a better opportunity for a safer, more secure, and more prosperous future.

Notes

1 Zemurray, known as "Sam the Banana Man," was a Russian Jewish immigrant who started with a few hundred dollars to become one of the wealthiest people in the United States.

2 Emily Perkins, *Coming to New Orleans: Four Items that Tell the story of Immigration Between World War I and the Civil Rights Act*, The Historic New Orleans Collection, Sept. 12, 2023, https://www.hnoc.org/publications/first-draft/coming-new-orleans-four-items-tell-story-immigration-between-world-war-i.

3 Anderson, Thomas P., *The War of the Dispossessed: Honduras and El Salvador, 1969*, Lincoln, (University of Nebraska Press 1981).

4 Mohamad Moslimani, Luis Noe-Bustamante and Sono Shah, *Facts on Hispanics of Honduran Origin in the United States, 2021*, Pew Research Center, Aug. 16, 2023, https://www.pewresearch.org/hispanic/fact-sheet/us-hispanics-facts-on-honduran-origin-latinos/#:~:text=From%202000%20to%202021%2C%20the,2000%20to%20700%2C000%20in%202021.

5 Moslimani et al., *Facts on Hispanics of Honduran Origin in the United States, 2021*.

6 The section on the Bajo Aguan Valley drew extensively from Aviva Chomsky's *Central America's Forgotten History: Revolution, Violence, and the Roots of Migration* as well as the report from Human Rights Watch entitled, "*There Are No Investigations Here": Impunity for Killings and Other Abuses in Bajo Aguán, Honduras*.

7 *Economic Survey of Latin America and the Caribbean (Honduras) 2009–2010*, Economic Commission for Latin America and the Caribbean, https://repositorio.

cepal.org/server/api/core/bitstreams/1004d176-0a26-4831-ae95-aeefce256405/content.
8 *Economic Survey of Latin America and the Caribbean (Honduras) 2009–2010.*
9 *Economic Survey of Latin America and the Caribbean (Honduras) 2009–2010.*
10 Brett Heinz, *Honduras: Social and Economic Indicators After 12 Years of National Party Rule*, Center for Economic and Policy Research, Feb. 4, 2022, https://www.cepr.net/honduras-social-and-economic-indicators-after-12-years-of-national-party-rule/.
11 Heinz, *Honduras: Social and Economic Indicators After 12 Years of National Party Rule.*
12 Ben Corson and Jeffrey Hallock, *Intersecting Crises: Pandemic and Hurricanes Add to Political Instability Driving Migration from Honduras*, Migration Policy Institute, June 10, 2021, https://www.migrationpolicy.org/article/pandemic-hurricanes-political-instability-migration-honduras.
13 Corson and Hallock, *Intersecting Crises: Pandemic and Hurricanes Add to Political Instability Driving Migration from Honduras.*
14 Corson and Hallock, *Intersecting Crises: Pandemic and Hurricanes Add to Political Instability Driving Migration from Honduras.*
15 *Economic Analysis of the Honduras Remittances Ecosystem*, USAID, 2022, https://pdf.usaid.gov/pdf_docs/PA00Z69J.pdf.
16 *Economic Analysis of the Honduras Remittances Ecosystem.*
17 *Intentional homicides (per 100,000 people) – Honduras*, The World Bank, https://data.worldbank.org/indicator/VC.IHR.PSRC.P5?locations=HN.
18 *Intentional homicides (per 100,000 people) – Honduras.*
19 Nicole Ward and Jeanne Batalova, *Central American Immigrants in the United States*, Migration Policy Institute, May 10, 2023, https://www.migrationpolicy.org/article/central-american-immigrants-united-states.
20 *In 2022, At Least 4,050 Women Were Victims of Femicide in Latin America and the Caribbean: ECLAC*, Economic Commission for Latin American and the Caribbean, Nov. 23, 2023, https://www.cepal.org/en/pressreleases/2022-least-4050-women-were-victims-femicide-latin-america-and-caribbean-eclac#:~:text=Of%20the%2019%20countries%20and,Salvador%20and%20Uruguay%20(1.6).
21 *Number of femicides in Honduras in 2023, by month*, Statista Research Department, Mar. 5, 2024, https://www.statista.com/statistics/1133354/number-femicides-month-honduras/.
22 *Segundo Informe sobre la impunidad en homicidios*, Alianza por La Paz y la Justicia (APJ), June 4, 2019, https://www.flipsnack.com/asjhonduras/segundo-informe-de-impunidad-en-homicidios.html.
23 *Honduras: Responding to multiple crises to prevent violence against women*, UN Women, April 19, 2022, https://untf.unwomen.org/en/stories/news/2022/04/honduras-responding-to-multiple-crises-to-prevent-violence-against-women.
24 Colleen Putzel-Kavanaugh and Ariel G. Ruiz Soto, *Shifting Patterns and Policies Reshape Migration to U.S.-Mexico Border in Major Ways in 2023*, Migration Policy Institute, Oct. 2023, https://www.migrationpolicy.org/news/border-numbers-fy2023.
25 Putzel-Kavanaugh and Ruiz Soto, *Shifting Patterns and Policies Reshape Migration to U.S.-Mexico Border in Major Ways in 2023.*

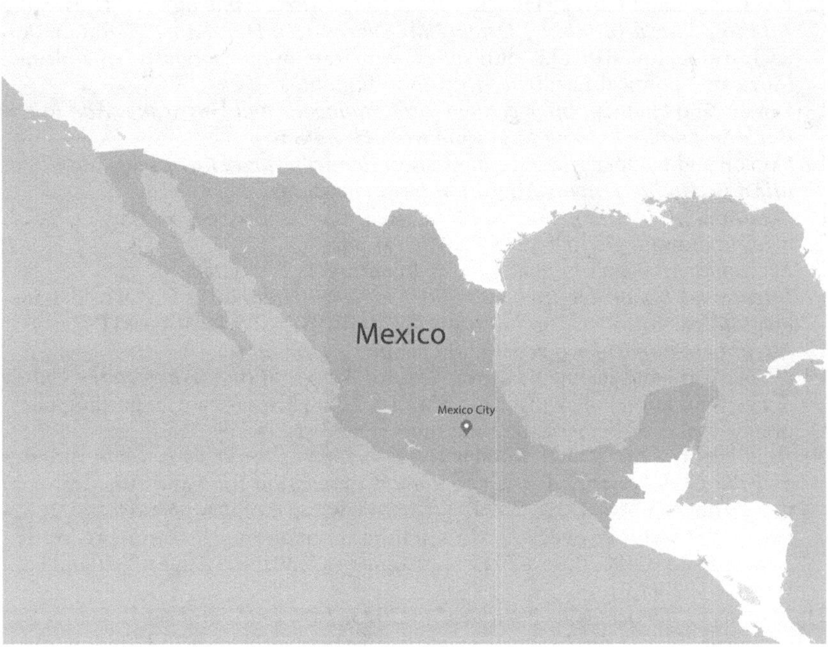

MAP 6.1 Mexico

DISTANCE TO US BORDER: 0 MILES

OBSTACLES TO TRAVEL TO THE UNITED STATES: SONORAN DESERT, PARTIALLY BUILT WALL

Source: Captian.N/Shutterstock

6

MEXICO

Beyond the Wall

The United States and Mexico share a 1,900-mile border and the most robust trade network of any two countries on earth: As of September 2023, Mexico and the United States exchanged approximately $800 billion in bilateral trade, making Mexico the United States's leading trade partner.

How then can politicians and other uninformed individuals call for a figurative and literal sealing off of the border between the two nations? Such a move would certainly harm the US economy, which helps explain why nether political party in the United States has really explored or attempted to "build the beautiful wall." Most commerce/trade, it should be noted, passes through established "ports of entry," i.e., highways and official checkpoints.

Others tell us that Mexico is stealing from and exploiting the United States; Mexican nationals in the United States and their descendants (and others) sent approximately $56 billion (in 2022) to Mexico. These remittances represent approximately 2 percent of Mexico's $2.6 trillion economy. But critics of these capital flows forget to mention that those dollars eventually flow back to the United States in the form of tourism (Mexicans are leading foreign tourists to the United States—though Canadians accounted for 28 percent of all tourist arrivals to the United States in 2022). Mexicans buy real estate in the United States among other purchases. Capitalism functions—though neither of the authors of this book are formally trained economists—through the constant churn of dollars/capital, a reality theorized and then actualized by the Scottish economist John Maynard Keynes early in the 20th century.

DOI: 10.4324/9781003357605-7

Now, as we write, some of the most extreme elements in our nation are calling for the invasion of Mexico in order to control irregular border crossings and stem the flow of fentanyl. Respected Yale historian and author Greg Grandin published a chilling essay in *The New York Times* on November 1, 2023, titled "The Republicans who want to invade Mexico." The writer laid out the entire arc of the story, starting with the Trump Administration, which floated the idea of secretly shooting US missiles into Mexico (and hoping the Mexicans wouldn't notice where they originated). Trump was quickly disavowed of this absurdity by more seasoned, rational members of his administration. But Grandin reminds us of the multiple invasions by the United States of our neighbor to the south, including the 1846 invasion which resulted in Mexico losing 51 percent of its national territory: the United States gained a third of what's referred to as the continental United States.

This chapter, like the other chapters in this book, seeks to explain the movement of people from the nation of Mexico to the United States. Economics, proximity, and shared culture and values explain much of the migratory process. In 2021, Mexican nationals numbered 10.7 million individuals in the United States, a number that has been on the decline recently as Mexicans return to their nation of origin as a result of political and social pressures in the United States and the dramatic effects of the COVID-19 pandemic. Yet, Mexicans (in 2021) made up 34 percent of the recent Hispanic immigrant population and were the largest group; they are also—according to Pew Research—the largest group (24 percent) of all US immigrants.

We plan to trace the historic evolution of an economic, geographic, and political pattern that has led to "the border" as we know it. The news and images of individuals seeking to cross into the United States from the global south (through Mexico) represent a curse to many that must be controlled. Others—those seeking easy access to cheap labor—view this situation as nothing short of a blessing and windfall. A windfall that other nations—such as Japan—can never enjoy due to constraints of geography, culture, and tradition.

The Historic Arc

When the Spaniards, under the direction of Hernán Cortés, conquered the Aztec Empire in a military campaign that lasted from 1519 to 1521, the United States of America, it is important to remember, did not exist. The Spaniards named their new overseas territory "New Spain"—a land mass that extended roughly from today's Guatemala to Oregon, bounded East-West by the Rocky Mountains and the Pacific Ocean. About 100 years later, in the early days of the 17th century, English and Dutch settlers would establish colonies in Virginia, New York, and Plymouth, Massachusetts—among other places—and the French would settle at Quebec and Montreal.

Independence from European masters would occur in the late 18th century (the 13 English colonies along the US Eastern Seaboard broke away from England between 1776 and 1783), and 27 years later, influenced by the scrappy American colonists and the rhetoric/reality of the 1789 Revolution in France, Mexico declared its independence from Spain. The September 16, 1810, "Grito de Dolores" is the Mexican independence cry—literally the "Shout from [the town of] Dolores."

The Mexican independence process ended in 1821 with a failed attempt to create "a Mexican Empire" under Agustín de Iturbide; he was quickly deposed and the *caudillo* leader, Antonio López de Santa Anna, would dominate politics, the military, and society for the next 30 years.

At this time, Mexican society was centered in and around Mexico City; vast mineral wealth and a fertile agricultural setting allowed the Spaniards to flourish and grow wealthy over a 300-year colonial period. Much of the area north of the city was a sort of "no man's" land—loosely populated through the construction of *presidios* (military forts) and Franciscan missions—one of which (at San Antonio, in current-day Texas), Misión San Antonio de Valero, protected by Presidio de Béjar—is also known more colloquially in the United States as "The Alamo."

The Anglos Move In

In the 1820s, having secured independence from Spain, the Mexican government at Mexico City "invited" settlers from east of the Mississippi River into Texas—which they controlled. The idea was that settlement by Anglos would help develop the area and prevent intrusions from nomadic Native Americans and others. Settlers would have to agree to obey the Constitution of Mexico and the principles/orders and traditions of the Roman Catholic Church. In exchange they could move in and farm the land. Stephen Austin took advantage of this Mexican goal of "populating" the area, and the Tejanos moved to the area that is today called Austin, Texas.

In 1833, the Mexican leader Santa Anna dissolved the Mexican constitution of 1824, and tensions between the Anglo settlers and the Mexican government intensified. The Mexicans realized by early 1830 that the Americans outnumbered them in Texas; the Anglos were reluctant to obey the dictator Santa Anna, who ruled without a recognizable constitution. The conflict that developed occurred at the site of the Presidio/Mission in San Antonio—"The Alamo."

The events of 1836 are fairly well known; that's the year that Santa Anna marched on San Antonio to put down a rebellion by the Anglo settlers, who had declared independence from Mexico on March 2 of that year. Santa Anna won the battle at the Alamo: virtually all of the Anglo defenders of the fort were slaughtered—187–257—though Santa Anna's rag-tag adolescent army suffered perhaps 600 deaths, about one-third of his assault force. A few days later, at San Jacinto, Santa Anna was captured, ransomed after he signed a declaration of Independence for Texas. Upon returning south, he declared the document null and void, since it was signed under duress.

"The Texas Question" lingered in the United States for the next eight years. Northerners were suspicious of the motives of southerners who wanted to annex Texas, suggesting they only wanted to do so to advance the agricultural economy with its cruel ancillary labor system, chattel slavery.

The election of southerner and expansionist James K. Polk (from Tennessee) to the presidency in 1844 changed everything. He was determined to settle the Texas question and did so by essentially invading the sovereign nation to the south, Mexico. In 1846, a border dispute between the two nations put US soldiers in contested territory; those soldiers were fired upon and killed, and war was declared against Mexico by the United States.

The war lasted a year and a half, and Mexico City was occupied by the United States —the United States final assault was at the city's highest point, Chapultepec Hill. There, the legend of the "Niños Héroes" (heroic boys) was born—six young boy soldiers wrapped themselves in the Mexican flag and dramatically jumped to their deaths rather than surrender to the American soldiers.

The war ended with the treaty of Guadalupe Hidalgo of 1848. The Mexicans—desiring that the Americans leave them alone—signed the document on the condition that once signed, the Americans would vacate Mexico. The Americans left, but took half the Mexican land area with them: Literally 51 percent of Mexico fell into American hands—including what today we call the states of Texas, New Mexico, Arizona, California, Nevada, Colorado, Wyoming, Kansas, Oklahoma, and parts of Utah and Montana. The treaty transferred the land, and a payment by the United States (of $15 million) served as a sort of indemnity payment—allowing the United States to claim the land was "purchased."[1]

The current border between the United States and Mexico was set in 1854 via the "Gadsden Purchase"—a 29,000-square mile purchase (for $10 million) of a piece of territory extending out from the Mesilla Valley in New Mexico (West of Las Cruces) to Yuma, Arizona; the strip included all the land in and around Tucson and extended up almost to the territory that forms the city of Phoenix.

With the border set, both countries would drift apart, focusing on distinct issues: In the United States, tensions would build over "slave states versus free states" and the tone/pace of modern economic development: The Northern Model stressed an industrialized economic system that employed "wage" labor; the southern model preferred an agricultural system and couldn't envision an economy (or society) without the anachronistic and increasingly harsh system of chattel slavery. A Civil War, fought between the northern states and the south, would ensue from 1861 to 1865; the northern model ultimately prevailed but at a cost of some 780,000 lives lost. The 13th, 14th, and 15th amendments to the Constitution changed the nature of American society by guaranteeing the end to slavery, citizenship to all peoples born on US soil, and the right to vote for all (males) 21 years or older.

Mexico's 19th-century civil war (or "The War of the Reform") ended the same year the US Civil War began. In Mexico, the issue involved how society would transform from arbitrary *caudillo* rule (under Santa Anna) to something more modern and progressive—rule by constitution, under the leadership of Benito Juárez. The conservatives and the Roman Catholic Church went to war to prevent the liberal, modern constitution of 1857 from taking effect. That constitution severely limited the historic power of the Roman Catholic Church: The Church lost their special *fuero* or privileges in courts and other matters, education was secularized, and the Church was forced to give up lands that were not specifically used for Church functions and activities.

The war, which ground to a stalemate but left Juárez in power, was followed by a surreal period in Mexican modern history: Essentially, the Church and conservatives invited the French in to take over their country and install a European Emperor in Mexico (Maximiliano, a Hapsburg from Vienna) on the condition that he would annul the Constitution of 1857 and return the Church's power, prestige, and land!

Maximiliano made it clear that he was uninterested in "internal" Mexican disputes and ruled until he was captured by Juárez's forces and executed in June 1867. Mexico had survived its most serious crisis since the American intervention and the pendulum swung (upon Juárez's death, in 1872) toward a "law and order" platform, under the leadership of Porfirio Díaz, a military commander who fought against the French intervention and emerged as the undisputed (though hardly democratic) leader of the nation. He ruled from the 1870s until his ouster in 1911.

During Díaz's rule, scholars write of a so-called Pax Porfiriana, or a Peace imposed by the Díaz regime. It was a brutal sort of peace. There was no discernable constitution, and people who disobeyed the leader's rules, particularly in the rural areas of the nation, were harshly dealt with by the leader's personal police force: the *rurales*. The brutality of the regime forced Mexicans to leave the nation and head north. Others were invited into the nation by the president, who was extremely interested in the economic and infrastructural development of his nation. The technicians—or *cientificos*—lived in Europe and the United States and were offered generous contracts to assist with mining, railroad construction, port works, and other basic development projects.

The Migration Begins

Thus, for purposes of this text, a somewhat mutually collaborative migration over the US-Mexican border formally begins at about this time. Americans saw investment opportunity in Mexico, and Mexico needed investment dollars, technical equipment, and expertise. Of course, the real story of immigration from Mexico to the United States began when the border between the two nations changed in 1845, via annexation of Texas, then in 1848, via the Treaty of Guadalupe Hidalgo. People living in Santa Fe, New Mexico, for example (a Spanish outpost, then a Mexican city post Mexican independence in the early 19th century) were suddenly (after 1848) ruled from Washington, not Mexico City. Many chose to cross the new border back into Mexico, but many others in the new "American" territory stayed put. Scholars, including Oscar J. Martínez, estimate that there were about 100,000 people living in the conquered territory at the time of the Guadalupe Hidalgo treaty.

The Porfirio Díaz dictatorship—a forty-year process—created such inequality that Mexico became two nations: One rural and almost medieval in its backwardness, the other connected to modern capitals like Washington, Paris, and London. Historian Bill Beezley discusses this dichotomy in his classic text *Judas at the Jockey Club*. When the 80-year-old dictator fled, after holding sham presidential elections in 1910, the nation soon erupted in Revolution.

The Revolution and the First World War Impact on Immigration

The Mexican Revolution lasted about ten years, left one million to one and a half million dead and displaced an additional one million. The total population of Mexico at the time was 14 million. Most of those who fled, fled north. They arrived in places that had once been Mexican national territory—to cities such as Brownsville, Tucson, San Diego, and Los Angeles.

The Revolution occurred at the same time as the First World War, and both events, but especially the latter, would forever change Americans' perception of immigration and immigration law. In fact, the first national comprehensive immigration law was passed by congress in 1924 in response to the war. The goal at the time was focused on restricting the arrival of people from former enemy nations—Italy, Germany, and territories that comprised the former Ottoman Empire. Russians were singled out for exclusion due to the Revolution that rocked that massive territory starting in 1917.

Mexico and its revolution were not viewed as any sort of existential threat to the United States, and, thus, in the legislation passed in 1924 to set "quotas" for immigrants from certain places in the world, the Western Hemisphere (including, of course, Mexico) was not even mentioned. Italians, Russians, and Germans were the real problem for America, according to 1920s logic—and legislation.

But certainly many Mexican nationals—given the Revolution, coupled with general political/economic instability in the nation—migrated north and settled along the border with Texas, in Tucson as well as San Diego and the expanding city of Los Angeles. The "roaring twenties" in the United States defined a postwar period of prosperity and optimism, against the backdrop of anti-immigrant hysteria and the first of two [anti-Communist] "red scares." But the 1920s red scare, coupled with prohibition legislation ushered in via the 19th amendment to the constitution, were designed to keep out immigrants, especially from Germany, Italy, and other nations with "drinking culture" as well as Russians who had recently carried out a violent Marxist/Leninist-inspired revolution.

The "roaring twenties," built on much speculation and unreliable, untested economic formulations, came crashing down in October 1929. The so-called Great Depression resulted in widespread misery and unemployment for Americans—as much as 40 percent of the labor force lost their livelihood during this grim period. President Herbert Hoover (1928–1932) refused to admit that any of his policies had contributed to the crash, and the nation anxiously waited for new leadership. That leadership arrived after a long three years in March 1933, as the new administration of Franklin Delano Roosevelt took office.

Mexicans: Pulled in, Pushed out

The number of Mexicans living in the United States at this time is difficult to determine because, before the comprehensive immigration reform of 1924, immigrants were only counted when arriving at "Maritime ports of entry," which means that Mexicans who arrived by land went uncounted. The border patrol was set up at this time and crossing stations were established along the US southern border with Mexico and in the north along the border with Canada. The 1929 economic collapse led to all sorts of nationalist policies, including what could be called essentially a "dragnet" against Mexican nationals and their children (i.e., US citizens, as determined by the 14th amendment to the US Constitution). The severe unemployment after October 1929 was attributed, to some degree, to a preponderance of Mexicans in the nation, and many—as many as a million—were simply rounded up and deported. This was indeed a low-point in US-Mexican relations.

President Roosevelt's policies (after 1933) based on a Keynesian economic perspective (widespread and massive spending from the government) helped reactivate the US economy. The start of the Second World War in September 1939 also helped.

The United States' entrance in this war, which occurred after the Japanese attack at Pearl Harbor on December 7, 1941, required an adjustment in US policy toward Mexico (and Latin America in general). The United States desperately needed Latin American collaboration for the war effort in the form of access to cheap and plentiful raw materials—oil, quartz, balsa wood, cotton, sugar, coffee, and tin were just a few of the primary products imported into the United States for the war economy. The most important "product" of course, was labor; the Mexican laborers recently deported (in 1929–1933) now needed to return, and they did so under a new federal program (established in 1942) called the "Bracero Program."

Why would Mexicans return to a place from which they had recently been deported, illegally and violently in many cases? Better and more secure wages help explain this seemingly paradoxical situation. "Bracero" was contracted labor, with an established wage, and the program offered housing. The workers performed, essentially, agricultural work that could not be performed by American workers who were called up for both military service and factory work to build the war infrastructure that helped defeat the Axis powers by 1945.

"Bracero" lasted longer than the war, suggesting a continual need for low-wage labor along the border, and in the United States in general. The program eventually ended, but not until 1964. A new era had begun—the 1960s—one marked by a renewed concern for Civil Rights—rights bestowed on citizens and residents, which allowed them to function, fully, in a modern, progressive society. Bracero, since it never offered citizenship or long-term residency, was considered anachronistic, abusive, and out of step at this time—especially after the passage of the landmark 1964 Civil Rights legislation in the United States.

The next "event" that focused attention on US-Mexican immigration and border concerns occurred in the 1960s when the Mexican government took the initiative to corral labor at the border. The "Programa de Industrialización Fronteriza" was begun in 1964, designed to correspond to the reality at the border: an expanding market in the north (the United States), existing in close proximity with workers who could not be fully employed or engaged by the Mexican government. Building factories along the border in Mexico, particularly in Matamoros, Nuevo Laredo, Reynosa, Ciudad Juárez, and Tijuana, would solve two (or three) problems simultaneously: Inexpensive Mexican labor could productively work in factories and finished (or near finished) goods could easily be shipped back to market (in the United States). The labor would never actually have to set foot in the United States, and finally, this entire "system" would/could undercut the strength and protections of US labor unions, which were, at this time, at their apex.

The Maquiladora System

Building on the success—for the capitalists and the governments of Mexico and the United States —of the *maquiladora* industry (a *maquiladora* is essentially an assembly plant, a high labor-intensive factory) workers, plus people in general began moving toward the border (to the cities mentioned above) to take advantage of direct and indirect employment offered by the plants. During this time in the United States, under the presidency of Ronald Reagan, who understood the need for labor from the "global south," the Immigration Reform and Control Act (IRCA) was passed through congress and signed by the president. The previous comprehensive reform from 1965, also known as "Hart-Celler," restricted Mexican "legal" immigration to 18,200 yearly; together with other restrictions from the 1980 Refugee Act (which allowed people with a "credible fear of persecution" to seek refugee status in the United States)—all of these policies and historic realities meant that Mexicans, who share a 1,954 mile border with the United States, simply crossed into the nation to the north.

In the United States, they lived in the shadows, worked in US agriculture and factories, and contributed to federal tax rolls by using the Taxpayer Identification Number (TIN) program established by the IRS in 1996. These TINs allowed people who were unauthorized to work in the United States to pay into the Social Security and Medicare systems, affording them "a minimum" level of legality in the United States. But the sense in the nation at this time (just like now) was that the nation was being "overwhelmed" with undocumented peoples. The Democratic Congress and the Republican president responded, as noted above, by signing a sweeping immigration reform in 1986—the last time a comprehensive immigration package has been passed in our nation.

NAFTA

Then came NAFTA. During the Reagan administration (1980–88) and especially during the follow-on administration of President George H.W. Bush, the political and social priorities in the Americas favored an "integrative" approach modeled after the European Union: A giant free trade zone was envisioned, linking the three largest economies in North America: the United States, Canada, and Mexico. The negotiations over NAFTA created much consternation, especially in the United States. Many senators (the Senate approves international treaties) balked at combining the US economy with the Mexican economy—perceived to be weak and underdeveloped.[2] Texas billionaire and entrepreneur Ross Perot, running for the presidency in 1992, spoke of a "Giant Sucking Sound" that he imagined if NAFTA were to be implemented. He was referring, of course, to the sound of labor moving from the industrial Midwest of the United States toward and to Mexico—where labor costs were much lower, and laborers were not protected by Union concerns or federal (US) government regulations.

Perot, who did not win the 1992 presidency, wasn't wrong. Many well-paying, middle-class factory jobs migrated south, and entire towns in Indiana, Ohio, Wisconsin, and Kentucky disappeared. NAFTA was designed to help factory owners cut costs, deliver more and more economical goods to North American consumers and stem the flow of labor from Mexico to the United States. People in Mexico could migrate north (within Mexico) and work in the rapidly multiplying factories along the border.

On the day NAFTA was implemented, 1 January 1994, a disturbance broke out in the south of Mexico: On that day, the EZLN—Ejercito Zapatista para la Liberación Nacional (Zapatista National Liberation Army)—appeared in the southern part of the nation, Chiapas, and surrounding areas, arguably the poorest, most forgotten region of Mexico.

The uprising garnered immediate international attention and played into the hands of critics of the treaty: i.e., it was unwise and counterproductive to negotiate with a violent, backwards nation like Mexico. The leader of the group, the mysterious (at the time) "Sub-comandante Marcos," was a university philosophy professor who understood the long, unequal, racist nature of his society. He released his platform (and the platform of the Zapatista army), and the world attempted to absorb the history and philosophy lessons imparted from the south of Mexico. In his "First Declaration from the Lacandon Jungle—today we say '*ya basta*'" ["enough already"], the philosopher wrote, "we are the product of 500 years of struggle…first against slavery, then during the War of Independence against Spain…" and the story went on and on. Essentially, Marcos, *nom de guerre* of Rafael Sebastían Guillén Vicente, pointed out an inconvenient reality in the post-NAFTA world: Mexico had never really been free, independent, democratic, or fair regarding the manner by which resources were allocated, and in terms of a winners-take-all system (the capitalists, landowners, and their friends) and the losers (the people) get nothing.

The same year, the people of California passed a referendum, Proposition 187, led by the then governor Pete Wilson—a man with clear presidential ambitions, now a mere footnote in history. The proposition, also known as the "Save our State Initiative," offered unusual cruelty to people living in the state without proper documentation. For example, by Proposition 187, school children would be denied access to public school unless they could prove they were properly documented. Doctors were told they could only treat the documented.

The "heroes" of this time period were the public school teachers and physicians—and of course many others. The teachers cited *Plyler v. Doe*, the 1982 Supreme Court Case that determined the unconstitutionality of withholding funds, or education, from any child in America—even an undocumented child. The doctors simply refused to enforce Proposition 187, explaining that their oath was called the Hippocratic Oath—to do no harm—and the California ballot initiative ran contrary to that ancient obligation. The Proposition ended up before the California Supreme Court, where it was declared, by 1999, unconstitutional, and it disappeared.

Proposition 187 came from blue/ish California. While that state has been at the forefront of many cool Hollywood inspired-trends and relaxed beach vibes, it has also generated some really terrible legislation. Proposition 187 politically energized and mobilized Hispanics in the state, ended Governor Wilson's national ambitions, and turned a sort of red state bright blue. California, we should remember, is a significant site of defense contractors. Additionally, two major military bases—one Naval at San Diego and another, Marine, based at Oceanside 50 miles to the north—influenced the economy and culture of southern California. Much of the defense industry dried up, or changed, after the fall of the Soviet Union in 1991. This meant unemployment for wide sectors of the middle class in America: engineers, salespeople, architects, scientists—they either had to move away, retool, or change their lifestyles. It was much easier to blame their troubles not on global economic and sociopolitical change but on "the Mexicans."

The California Hysteria Spreads

The rage and hysteria unleashed in California in the early 1990s foreshadowed what was to come in America. In 2010, Arizona's governor Jan Brewer signed SB 1070, the "show me your papers bill" as it became known. It allowed law enforcement to ask for people's "papers"—immigration status—at routine traffic stops, i.e., it authorized racial and ethnic profiling, something contrary to the American ethos. Brewer, after famously waving her finger in the face of then sitting President Barack Obama as he stepped off Air Force One in Phoenix in 2013, has all but disappeared from the political scene.

Up next, Alabama: HB 56 passed in 2011 and not only copied the Arizona legislation but went further and criminalized anyone "helping" an undocumented person. Read literally, the law meant that an American citizen could be jailed for taking an injured undocumented person to the emergency room. The good people of Alabama pushed back, and by 2013, the law had been all but gutted by the courts. The law was very inconvenient for wealthy agricultural interests in the state: After the law passed, their labor force left the state, leaving them with billions of dollars in losses.

The candidacy (and presidency) of Donald Trump emerged out of this. Mr Trump focused unprecedented attention on Mexican immigrants, referring to them (on the day he announced his candidacy in the summer of 2015) as "rapists and murderers." It was a moment that many predicted (including the authors of this text) would dissipate together with the candidate. Rather, the message resonated with a wide sector of the American public, and Mr Trump went on to win the presidency against the establishment candidate, Hilary Clinton.

Trump tried, during his four tempestuous years in the presidency, to eliminate Deferred Action for Childhood Arrivals (DACA) protections for people eligible for the Obama-era program; the case went to the Supreme Court, but the Court rejected Trump's feeble attempt at overturning the popular program. He referred to folks who held Temporary Protective Status (TPS) as originating from "shithole" countries, and he spoke of building a "Big, beautiful wall" along the Southern United States border. The wall was never completed, especially after 2018 when Democrats regained the House of Representatives and refused to appropriate the funding. A "wall" has never served as deterrent for people hoping to remake their lives and improve the lives of loved ones left behind in Mexico, Central America, and the rest of the world.

Now, the Biden Administration (in late 2023) seems to be backsliding to Trump Era policies; he's begun construction of a segment of the "Wall," and his administration is considering permanent/draconian restrictions on asylum in order to placate his political opponents, who (as of this writing in early 2024) are using the migrant situation to hold up aid to Ukraine and Israel.

People continue to come here—to the United States —and if they arrive by land, without documentation, they generally arrive from the South (via Mexico) rather than through Canada, from the North. The essential question of "why" people continue to come here is complicated but related to historic / cultural factors, i.e., the United States has always been perceived as a welcoming, safe-haven for migrants. People migrate here to try and improve their standard of living: the social mobility (albeit in decline in recent years) found in the United States is not really present in Honduras,

Haiti, Cuba, and other places in the Americas. People do not want to accept their status as "stuck in poverty forever" and move accordingly. Many Mexicans view that border as an opportunity rather than a barrier. We can build the wall higher, but as long as conditions in the global south remain extremely unequal and violent, people will carry longer ladders to circumvent the wall. Only collaboration between the United States and Mexico/Central America and the other nearby "sending nations," together with an act of congress, i.e., bipartisan comprehensive immigration reform, will diminish the flow, bring order to a chaotic situation, and help people who hope to remake their lives in this nation. At this time in history, America desperately needs the labor, youthful energy, and creativity that the vast majority of these migrants bring to this nation of immigrants.

The Push/Pull Factors

Mexican nationals know the broad outlines of US immigration policy and how it affects them directly and indirectly. Mexicans understand the contributions they've made to the success, development, and stability of US society. Most grudgingly accept the historic reality of an unjust, "land grab" referred to in the United States as "The Mexican American War," but in Mexico it's called "The War of North American aggression." They also understand that the first comprehensive immigration law of the United States, Johnson-Reed of 1924, wholly excluded the Western Hemisphere and focused on people who had been actual enemies of the United States (Germans, Italians, and people from the former Ottoman Empire) or perceived enemies (Russians, who staged a dramatic in-house revolution from 1917 to 1921).

Mexicans were harshly treated by US authorities when the US economy collapsed in 1929. About a million Mexicans, many of whom had sought safe harbor in the United States during and after the devastating Revolution there (1910–1920), were simply deported. Many of the children of these immigrants, US citizens via the 14th amendment to our constitution, were also deported.

The Bracero Program (1942–1964) was beneficial to both the United States and Mexico but offered another example of the more powerful partner (the United States) taking advantage of Mexico (for labor needs) and then canceling the partnership when the convenience of the relationship became inconvenient. "Bracero," in the new Civil Rights conscious era of the United States (the 1960s) did not intersect neatly with the new order which stressed equal rights for all, and governmental commitment to upholding fair labor standards for all. Bracero was essentially a pragmatic, unequal guest worker program that functioned during the war years, but, by the 1960s, had become outdated and anachronistic.

Next the industrialists and significant financial actors on both sides of the border created a new system to achieve the goals of "Bracero" while leaving the people in Mexico in place. The so-called Border Industrialization Program emerged and placed assembly plants along the border. Mexican nonunionized workers could work there for wages that were significantly above the Mexican minimum but certainly not at or close to US minimum wage. Nor were any union protections offered and the places where the workers moved—Reynosa and Matamoros, Ciudad Juárez, and Tijuana—proved grim, without adequate infrastructure or social structure. They became the sites of high homicide, smuggling of humans and drugs, and hundreds of unresolved cases of crimes against women, the femicide crisis that continues to plague that region of Mexico. Molly Molloy, a researcher who worked at New Mexico State University, insists that "impunity" is the real issue: Crimes committed against poor people, sex workers, and/or workers with no family contacts, connections, or friends tend to go unreported, or they're investigated "lightly" or not at all.

The Border Industrial Program and then the brutal, bruising debate surrounding NAFTA and "Free trade" in the early 1990s plus criminal activity/murder at the border all coalesced and built an "anti-Mexico" faction within the United States that culminated in the California legislation mentioned above. Mexicans will continue to come here provided the wealthiest nation in the world coexists next to and shares a border with a far less wealthy—a middle-income—nation of 128 million people.

About 60 percent of all Latinos living in the United States are Mexican. There are vast, significant, historic ties between the United States and Mexico. Closing off the United States to Mexico would require a Senate vote to annul NAFTA, and would have ruinous consequences for the US economy. The alternative approach—the only viable approach—would require congressionally approved, comprehensive immigration reform to bring the US labor needs in alignment with the immigrant flow toward the United States. It wouldn't be a perfect solution, but it would be much better than the images currently in the press and the politicization of a serious humanitarian crisis, replete with violence, murder, and death in the Sonoran Desert and surrounding areas.

The Migrants

The stories of those who have migrated here from Mexico are too numerous to recount here. Some people shared their stories with us, including a 21-year-old, living in the United States and studying at a small college in the US South. Adam Reyes was born in Tultitlan, Mexico, a suburb of the enormous Distrito Federal—the D.F.—or the capital city of Mexico. He walked, as a five-year-old, with his parents and his brother: "I remember holding my dad's hand, and my older brother's hand during the journey. Me and my ten-year-old brother were the only children making the journey with a group of adults."[3]

Like many migrants, this group of travelers was stopped in the United States and returned to Mexico, without any formal hearing, documentation, or official record. They decided to continue the journey, i.e., to reenter the United States. "We were hidden by a family in the USA—in California—and then we took a van to Atlanta where my mother has family." In Mexico, young Adam recalls living with his grandparents; his mother worked as a secretary, his father could not find work.

Upon arrival in Atlanta, the young boy enrolled in pre-K and attended a new elementary school that had been built about the time of his arrival. He excelled at school, quickly picked up English, and speaks the language without an accent. Now, in the United States, his mother stays home to care for her two young children born in the United States (she also cleans homes a couple times per week with a friend) and the father works in construction, and at a food truck on weekends. Adam's older brother also works in construction.

Adam is a DACA recipient and has to reapply for DACA status every two years at a cost of some $600:

> I'd like to stay here in the USA and I have lots of friends at the college, but very few people know about my status except my soccer coach and the folks in financial aid office. I want to find work after completing my degree, earn money and help my parents pay off the house they purchased five years ago. Then, they can come live with me when they grow older, and I can take care of them, the way they've taken care of me.

Susana Vélez is a 23-year-old college graduate living in small city in Tennessee with her mother, sister, and nephew. She arrived in the United States in 2000 from Mexico City, where she was born. Her father, who had owned small businesses in Mexico, had run into economic difficulties and "he didn't have influential friends," so there was no real opportunity to rebuild the business. He decided to travel, legally by plane, to the United States with the family.

The family fortunes changed with a devastating diagnosis of cancer for the father who, uninsured, was unable to secure proper medical treatment in the United States. He left for Mexico, and his wife promised that she would raise the two daughters in the United States. The family, by this point, had overstayed their 90-day tourist visas. "The last time I saw my dad was at the airport, when he returned to Mexico."[4]

After Susana's dad left, the family literally had no place to live and was living on the streets of their new city in America—a small city in western Tennessee. "My mother was so desperate that she thought of calling the police and asking them to deport us."

Susana excelled at school and was told by her mother that education represented freedom. Before graduating from high school, she visited the assistant principal at her public high school to ask about scholarships to continue studying and the school official "didn't really have any suggestions." So, Susana decided to research on her own and found a program called "Golden Door Scholarship." She applied, and the college to which she eventually matriculated was a partner school with Golden Door, and Susana was offered a full tuition, four-year scholarship, plus room and board, books, and health insurance. It was the first time she ever had health insurance.

She graduated from college with dual degrees in history and international relations in 2022; prior to graduating she began working at "All Saints Immigration Services" in her hometown—this work, providing services to undocumented people, convinced her to study further—to become an immigration attorney; at the time of this interview, Susana had been accepted to a law school in western Tennessee.

More misfortune, however, visited the family: Susana's older sister was criminally assaulted, and the category of assault was one of 12 crimes that allowed the sister to apply for protection under the "U Visa" category—which protects people who have been harmed within the United States. Susana and her mother were pulled in under this unfortunate circumstance, and Susana became a legal permanent resident in 2018, and recently purchased a small home using her earnings from her work at "All Saints."

Noel Santamaria was born in Mexico City and arrived in the United States as a 21-year-old in 1997. He arrived with his brother and brother-in-law in Modesto, California, and worked in agriculture "in the fields"; Modesto, at this time, was grim and dangerous. He soon arrived in Naples, Florida, where he's lived ever since. One of his brothers had been living in Naples and told Noel of plentiful job opportunities in construction in this young and growing, sunny Florida "west coast" city. "I worked in the orange fields for two weeks, but that work is really difficult," and so the 22-year-old moved to the construction sector and learned basic carpentry, and currently "has a group of people" working under him.

His wife arrived here in 2005 with their child, who is now 27 years old and had protection under DACA. They have an American-born 17-year-old son, who is high school student in South Florida.

Noel pays taxes through a taxpayer identification number—or the Individual Taxpayer identification number (ITIN). So, like many undocumented people in the United States, Noel pays taxes, and pays into social security—a benefit he'll never "collect" in his old age. "My mother died recently in Mexico, and I couldn't attend the service." Technology has allowed migrants to stay connected in all corners of the world; the matrimonies and funerals, and baptisms and *quinceñeras*, which are part of the daily rhythm of life in Latin America. Noel explains, "the Zoom funeral is really something catastrophic...especially when it's your mother."

"People in this country," explained Mr Santamaria, referring to the United States, "they don't understand the sacrifices that the undocumented make to be here...they think we're here taking jobs away from American citizens and that's simply ... untrue." Now, as of May 2023, the situation for the undocumented in Florida has become especially difficult, with a new anti-immigrant law signed by Governor DeSantis. DeSantis signed the law to show "toughness" as his campaign for president took shape, but eventually (in January 2024) the campaign collapsed.

The law remains, and it's made life difficult for undocumented people; the fear of being pulled over while driving. Mr Santamaria has been here in the United States for 27 years, so he has a bank account, a license, and insurance. But the new law makes it a crime to "transport" people from other states into Florida under "human trafficking" penalties. It also makes it more difficult for immigrants to receive treatment at Florida hospitals—requiring hospitals to fill in a "citizenship" questions on Medicaid forms, and it doesn't recognize documents issued by other states to the undocumented.

"People are leaving the state of Florida," according to Noel and others. If enough people leave, and agricultural interests are hurt—as was the case in California under Proposition 187, and Alabama in 2010, the law will most likely be revoked. Cruelly cracking down on hardworking people (Noel works six days a week and rests on Sunday) for political gains has proven elusive. Governors Pete Wilson, who signed California's "Proposition 187," and Arizona's Jan Brewer assumed that such crackdowns would propel their political programs forward, but both, now, are forgotten footnotes and represent cautionary tales in how not to appeal to voters and the American public in general.

Notes

1 This story is nicely presented in Howard Zinn's classic text, *A People's History of the United States*, 1980, chapter 10.
2 Today, Mexico is the 14th largest economy in the world, and, in mid-2023, became the most significant (in terms of dollar amount) trade partner with the United States.
3 Interview with Mr Reyes on 3/3/23 in Tennessee, United States.
4 Interview with SV, December 2023, at Jackson Tennessee.

MAP 7.1 Venezuela

DISTANCE TO US BORDER: 1,367 MILES

OBSTACLES TO TRAVEL TO THE UNITED STATES: COLOMBIA, DARIÉN JUNGLE, CENTRAL AMERICA, MEXICO

Source: Captian.N/Shutterstock

7

VENEZUELA

The Dutch Disease and Decline

As we prepare this chapter in late 2023, about one quarter of the population of Venezuela—a once-wealthy South American nation with more proven oil reserves under its subsoil than any other nation on earth—have left. That translates to seven million Venezuelans migrating, mostly in the past seven years.

Most have headed to neighboring Colombia, which has been attempting to integrate their Andean "cousins" into the nation of 50 million. About 1.8 million Venezuelans, it is estimated, are currently in Colombia. Others have gone to every corner of Latin America—Peru, Argentina, and Chile. Many, of course, have made the long, harrowing journey to the United States, often with little other choice than to literally "walk" from Venezuela to the US Southern border. There are thousands of miles of distance separating the two places, plus the nearly impenetrable Darién Gap (separating Panama from Colombia—a dense, unforgiving jungle with no roads, rivers, or railroad lines); then there's the risk of extortion, kidnapping, or worse from the various active gangs along the way. Travel on top of *la bestia*—the train that runs south-north through Mexico toward the United States—is hardly comfortable, or safe.

Like the other chapters in this book, this chapter will open with a discussion of the recent history of Venezuela, with a focus on how a once-rich South American nation could lose, literally, one quarter of its population to out-migration. Then we will focus on specific policies that Venezuelans have accessed to migrate to the United States over the past 25 years or so. It's important to study this crisis by focusing on shifting US policies.

DOI: 10.4324/9781003357605-8

For example, in late September 2023, the Biden Administration announced that it would begin deporting Venezuelans who cross into the United States unlawfully. Some Venezuelans living in the United States do have temporary protective status (TPS). But the Venezuelan migration crisis—the largest out-movement of people in the Western Hemisphere—is further complicated (for the United States) based on the fact that the United States and Venezuela "barely" maintain diplomatic relations. The United States closed its embassy in Caracas in 2019.

Historian John V. Lombardi challenges us to take a holistic view when considering Venezuelan history. He worries that a "presentist" mentality continually shapes the perception of a people and place. Thus, the contemporary crisis—beginning more than a quarter century ago in 1989 with the so-called "Caracazo"—urban rioting and official military repression which left hundreds dead—is a small slice of the story. In 1989, the government reduced the subsidy on gasoline and raised the price on public transportation; this was in response to a decline in the international price of oil starting in the mid-1980s, oil constituting the largest share, by far, of the Venezuelan export sector. Seventy-six percent of all exports out of Venezuela over the past decade are petroleum-based products. In 2013, that number was a staggering 96 percent.

The 1989 rioting set up the current crisis, but—as noted by Lombardi—the roots of the problem date back to a colonial (Spanish) economic model which favored mono-crop exports, a slave labor society, and a mercantilist mindset designed to favor and enrich the metropole. After 1989, a young, left-leaning army captain, Hugo Chávez Frias, would come to dominate the discourse in the Andean, oil-saturated nation, albeit from prison. He served some time in jail for his role in a planned but unsuccessful military coup in 1992 against President Carlos Andrés Pérez. Chávez was eventually pardoned/released and went on to dominate politics and society from the end of the 20th century (1999) until his death from cancer in March 2013.

Some Background History

Unlike other colonial enterprises in the region—namely Mexico and Peru—Venezuela offered very little for the Spanish conquerors in terms of precious metals or easily identifiable and transportable wealth. Early on, the Spaniards searched for El Dorado—the fictitious city of gold that would make them instantly and fabulously wealthy—but El Dorado didn't exist. The monumental architecture and sedentary native populations of other places in the region were never found in Venezuela; the natives that did inhabit the area were subjugated by the Spaniards and/or forced to resettle under Spanish domination.

Wealth during the colonial period—roughly a 300-year time frame extending from 1500 to 1800—was generated through cattle raising and farming of *cacao* along the slopes of mountains; this is the primary product involved in chocolate production. Changing tastes in Europe (and a saturation of the chocolate market) encouraged the production of coffee, and Venezuela, like its neighbors in Colombia and Brazil, developed a robust coffee economy in the 19th century after independence.

The question of labor has been central to the history of Venezuela. The Spaniards viewed the territory of Venezuela as a sort of large farm from which they would derive most of the economic benefits. They, for all intents and purposes, enslaved the natives and brought in enslaved people directly from Africa through the nearby slave-trading city of Cartagena (in modern-day Colombia) and via the nearby Caribbean islands.

Independence changed, to some degree, the formula and logic of slavery; slavery was associated with the "colonial" past and didn't follow the ideology of the "universal declaration of the rights of man"—the French charter from 1789 upon which much of the ideology of Latin American independence was based. Liberty, freedom, brotherhood. Nowhere did it mention slavery!

Venezuela would come to play a central role in the independence process. The territory, to assist with the defenses of the Caribbean, was raised to the level of "Captaincy General" in 1777, which meant more Spanish infrastructure—and oversight—for the territory. One of the leading architects of Latin American independence, Simón Bolívar, was from Caracas, from one of the wealthiest plantation-owning families in the area.

It's important, in considering the totality of Venezuelan history, as suggested by Lombardi, to remind ourselves of the centrality of Bolívar in Venezuelan history, the Venezuelan dedication to independence, and the formidable army created during this time by Bolívar. He recruited cowboys of the Venezuelan/Colombian plains called *llaneros*. They were experienced horsemen, able to kill from the saddle, and they represented a formidable fighting force. Venezuela, from that point onward, has been characterized by a serious, dedicated military tradition. It should, thus, come as no surprise that (in recent times) a man from the military, Hugo Chávez, would command such outsized influence over the nation. Modern democracy in Venezuela, it should be noted, dates back only to 1958 with the ouster of Marcos Pérez Jiménez, a military dictator who ruled—with a triumvirate of military rulers—from 1948.

A long military tradition, an economic structure based (until the mid-19th century) on slave labor, plus ownership of most of the nation's arable land by a small group of white Spanish-descended people meant that Venezuela, unlike Argentina, Brazil, or the United States, seemed structurally inhospitable to immigration. That all changed when the nation struck oil and became, seemingly overnight, wealthy. That occurred in the early 20th century.

The 1920s witnessed the development of the petroleum industry in Venezuela, and the nation grew rich between 1950 and the 1980s; in the mid-1980s, with the collapse of international oil prices and a contraction of the global economy, Venezuela's fortunes declined substantially. During the "boom" period, there was a steady "in-migration" to the Andean nation. First, some Spaniards fled to Venezuela during the cruel days of the Spanish Civil War—1936–1939; in the post–Second World War period, others arrived from Europe—Portuguese and Italians. They were encouraged to migrate in order to help with the industrial/technical development of the nation during the dictatorship. White Europeans, during the late 19th and first part of the 20th century, were encouraged to migrate to Latin America on the very specious and racist notion that they would "improve" the racial stock in places like Brazil, Argentina, and Chile. Migration from Europe to Venezuela was "later" than migration to other places in Latin America given the peculiarities of Venezuelan society and economic development.

Colombians, struggling through a variety of political and economic crises during this time period, migrated en masse to Venezuela during the "Boom" days—the 1960s through the early 1980s. Colombians accepted low-wage work in Venezuela and were generally treated as second-class citizens, even though the history and culture of the two nations is deeply intertwined. The modern border between the two nations extends about 2,000 kilometers and is mostly open, ill-defined, and relatively easy to traverse. The exact number of Colombians who migrated to Venezuela during this time is difficult to quantify, but in the 1990s it is estimated that 75 percent of all migrants to Venezuela were of Colombian descent. In 1971, the boom years for Venezuela, 30 percent of the foreign population was Colombian. Spaniards, in that same year, made up 25 percent of the foreign population at about 149,000 persons.[1]

The Colombian-Venezuelan border has been a contested space for quite some time. Illegal cross-shipments of goods and fuel (gasoline in Venezuela, which is subsidized by the government, is as much as ten times cheaper than gasoline in Colombia), leading to a shady black market of sorts at Maicao, a border town in western Venezuela that connects to the Colombian Guajira, the strip of Colombian land that extends up and over Venezuela, ending in the Caribbean Sea.

People, too, cross this lengthy (mostly), wide, open border: during the days when Colombia experienced slow, unremarkable growth and economic development, there was a "great pull," as mentioned above, toward neighboring Venezuela—this was during the 1960s through the 1980s. The trend is now completely reversed: i.e., there are perhaps 1.8 million Venezuelans in Colombia—a relatively stable neighboring nation with a slow-moving economy that hasn't been subject to the "Boom and Bust" cycle of its neighbors. Venezuela experienced great wealth through its petroleum production and suffered from what's referred to in economics jargon as the "Dutch Disease." This "disease" is based on what happened to the Netherlands in the 1960s when oil was discovered there, in the North Sea. The distortion of the Venezuelan economy essentially translated into 50 percent of its gross domestic product (GDP) depending on oil exports, with oil representing 95 percent of all exports! This is the disease! Obviously, Venezuela was forced to import almost everything it needed, including foodstuffs (from nearby Colombia, in fact), and those who benefited from the infusion of cash—very few, as a percentage of the population—spent lavishly on luxury goods, apartments in foreign cities (such as Paris and Miami), and the entire economy was predicated upon oil exports, oil maintaining a certain price on the global market, and political stability abroad.

Naturally, the whole system collapsed when oil prices retracted starting in the mid-1980s. The Venezuelan economy demonstrated its severe vulnerabilities at this time resulting in street protests, which the security forces responded to with overwhelming force—during what's known as the 1989 "Caracazo." Hundreds died and the stage was set for the emergence of some "other" political arrangement represented by a wide turn left with the election of Hugo Chávez in 1998; he took possession of the government as president in 1999.

In the early days of Chávez's "Bolivarian Revolution," oil prices were high, and he was able to return some of the profits to the poor and lower middle class in the form of direct government payments. This tactic lowered the level of poverty in the nation and cemented his relationship with the nation's poor; it infuriated the wealthy who were accustomed to controlling the government. Chávez was part of a new, pan-Latin American so-called Pink Tide of leaders who did not support the status quo and saw their mission as lifting as many of their citizens out of poverty as possible. Mr Chávez was the indisputable leader of this group: he was brash, authoritarian, charismatic, and determined to derail traditional alliances and "business as usual" in the region. He founded the ALBA group in 2004 (with Cuba's Fidel Castro), and the 11-nation organization successfully defeated the US plan to create a "Free Trade Area of the Americas"; the ALBA leaders saw such an arrangement as simply another potential path to "Yanqui Imperialism."

Another leader of this so-called Pink Tide—another oil-producing nation in the region—was Ecuador under the leadership of Rafael Correa. Correa ruled for a decade, from 2007 to 2017; an economist who holds a PhD from a US university, the leftist leader managed to reduce poverty by

15 percent in the Andean nation. From 2006 to 2019, Evo Morales ruled in Bolivia as part of this movement and helped restore dignity and rights to indigenous people—he counted himself among them—which had long been ignored by the national government in a nation where the majority (perhaps as many as 70 percent of the population) is made up of Indigenous peoples.

The current president of Brazil, Luiz Inácio Lula da Silva, ruled the nation of 220 million souls from 2003 to 2011. Mr da Silva, "presided over an unprecedented era of economic and social growth in the nation," but the worldwide economic recession in 2008–2009 essentially collapsed the Brazilian "miracle."[2]

Remarkably, the Pink Tide—most vociferously championed by Chávez in Venezuela—worked for a while. The poor received direct benefits from economic growth and prosperity, which was tied to the strength of the export sector during this time. In other words, a reliance on business as usual—exports of primary products in all cases except the Brazilian—as a way of generating revenue. Venezuela, for example, never invested funds from oil profits to create a microchip industry. Brazil, on the other hand, broke out of this "Dependency" arrangement by insisting, during the era of Getúlio Vargas (who ruled from 1930 to 1945 and again from 1950 to 1954), that the nation needed to invest in heavy industry and manufacturing in order to become a world economic leader. Currently, Brazil is the world's ninth leading economy in the world and the second leading economy in the Americas—one place ahead of Canada.

The centrality of oil to the Venezuelan economy—discussed above—led to a major dispute between the mercurial Chávez and the Petróleos de Venezuela (PdVSA)—the state-run oil conglomerate. When PdVSA called for a strike as a way to force Chávez to commit to greater transparency and democracy, the president fired 18,000 workers, or 40 percent of the workforce. Given the importance of oil—which constituted at that time about 50 percent of the nation's GDP—this represented a bold move by the president and had long-lasting effects on oil output for the nation. Many fired workers left for other places—Houston, the Middle East, and nearby Colombia—and the Venezuelan state oil industry never really recovered. Colombia, with the help of Venezuelan engineers and other oil personnel who migrated to the neighboring Andean nation, enjoyed an oil boom in the aftermath of the Venezuelan strike. Currently, petroleum is the leading export of Colombia, representing about 45 percent of the nation's exports.

After this "move" in 2002/2003, Mr Chávez was both emboldened and drifted into a more authoritarian direction. In 2006, for example, he called US President George W. Bush "the devil" from the podium at the United Nations. He could do this because, during most of his regime, international oil prices were high, except for a brief dip in 2008, and the price recovered in 2009, only to collapse (dramatically) in 2014, a year after Chávez's death. But billions of dollars flowed to the president's pet project—the Bolivarian Missions—which subsidized the poor and helped lift millions of Venezuelans out of poverty. Sadly, once the price of oil faltered, the subsidies subsided.[3]

Then, in March 2013, Mr Chávez died of cancer, and his chosen successor Nicolás Maduro took over as president of the nation. Maduro, who is still the president of the nation as of this writing in October 2023, lacks the grace, charm, or intelligence of his predecessor, and the situation in Venezuela has spiraled downward, especially after the hostile Trump Administration took over in Washington, an administration that threatened to invade the Andean nation.

Naturally, people left. The biggest "push" factors out of Venezuela have been lackluster leadership, limited democracy, and an unclear future for the people. Long ago, those who had the means to leave the nation left, settling in France and Panama or Miami (the wealthy); a sizeable middle-class Venezuelan community developed about 30 years ago (after the Caracazo of 1989) just west of Fort Lauderdale in South Florida. Today, "Weston" is home to about 11,000 people from Venezuela; Venezuelans comprise the largest Hispanic group in the city of approximately 68,000 residents.

In recent times, Venezuelans have left for other places in Latin America and the world: There are approximately 2.8 million Venezuelans in Colombia as of October 2023 and 1.5 million in Peru as of June 2023. Hundreds of thousands have left for Brazil, Ecuador, Chile, and Argentina, and, as of June 2023, there were 124,000 Venezuelans in the Dominican Republic. The Dominican GDP (the total value of all goods and services produced by a nation) is about five times lower than that of Venezuela. This demonstrates, to some degree, the enormity of the sociopolitical crisis presently in Venezuela.

As for the United States, there are about 650,000 Venezuelans in the United States as of this writing. During the decade of Venezuelan crisis, 2010–2020, the population of Venezuelans tripled in the United States.

The Pull Factors

The factors that have driven Venezuelans toward the United States are varied, but inexorably related to the Venezuelan oil industry. Commercial production of petroleum began in 1914—the same year the First World War started—and US companies were offered concessions for exploration, development, and technology transfer. It's important to emphasize that Venezuela is estimated to sit on 17 percent of the world's proven petroleum reserves. In the early 1970s, during an oil embargo from the Middle East,

Venezuela was producing 3.7 million barrels per day; currently, the nation produces about 720,000 barrels, five times less than its 1970s levels. In 1976, Venezuela nationalized its oil industry under PdVSA to hold onto more of the profits generated by the oil industry; this is known, collectively as the "boom" period for the Venezuelan economy and society.

The decline for Venezuela's economy and society has been astounding. From 2014 to 2021, the economy shrank by 75 percent. The United States has imposed harsh sanctions, and there is little, if any, cooperation between oil companies operating in the United States and Venezuela. In 2019, the United States stopped receiving shipments of Venezuela crude—all of which has led to a massive immigration crisis.

As of this writing, approximately 7.5 million Venezuelans have left the nation. To put this number in perspective: Imagine 80 million Americans—people from the United States—leaving the nation within a relatively short period of time! But back in the 1970s, there was a lot of money gushing out of Venezuela. In April 1976, Air France initiated service between Paris and Caracas (via the Azores) on the Supersonic Concorde. Venezuelan students at the University of Miami (in Coral Gables, Florida) took advantage of the proximity of their Capital city, Caracas (2 hours and 20 minutes of flight time) to essentially "commute" to school. They left their Ferraris—according to one eye witness—parked in the sun on the campus. Venezuelan shoppers in Miami became known—during this time period, as the "Deme dos" crowd, "Give me two..." Many in the United States were contemptuous of this new-money excess and commented on how Venezuelan art buyers shopped by "the meter"—knowing nearly nothing about the artist or the genre of the art being purchased.

Of the millions of Venezuelans who are presently living in Colombia, many simply "walked" there and are referred to as "los caminantes," the walkers. The border between the two nations is long and porous, and tens of thousands of Venezuelans have continued their travel beyond Colombia, up through the Darién Gap (the unforgiving jungle region that separates Panama from Colombia).

The situation in Venezuela has gone from bad to worse. The "bad" began when the charismatic leader of the Andean nation died of cancer in March 2013; then oil prices sank, and the Bolivarian Missions project all but collapsed. The new national leader—Nicolás Maduro, a truck driver before entering the political arena—was hardly ready for prime time. Then Mr Trump's election changed the tenor of US foreign policy—turning it chaotic in an instant. After 2017, the United States (i.e., Trump) suddenly became fixated with dictators abroad and reached out to leaders in Russia and North Korea. He treated with disdain "lesser" dictators (those without rockets) such as Maduro and Daniel Ortega in Nicaragua. In 2018, presidential elections in Venezuela were held, returning Mr Maduro to the presidency by a wide margin. The Organization of American States (OAS; headquartered in D.C.), the United States, and others determined that irregularities in the election process (including changing the date twice) constituted fraud, and refused to recognize Maduro as the legitimate leader of the nation. Economic and political sanctions were applied, and by 2019 oil shipments were halted to the United States after the state-run oil conglomerate, PdVSA, was sanctioned. Those sanctions were lifted in late 2023, then reimposed 6 months later by the Biden Administration, as Maduro cracked down on opposition candidates. In the 2024 presidential election, Maduro was declared once again victorious. The opposition cited significant irregularities in the election process. Harvard professor, Steve Levitsky, as reported by the *New York Times* characterized the July 28th election as "one of the most egregious electoral frauds in modern Latin American history."

The Venezuelan exodus has been stunning—again, as of this writing, approximately one quarter of the nation's population has left—and the United States has not been prepared for their arrival to the US southern border. The political rhetoric in the United States has been accusatory, with each side (Republicans and Democrats) accusing the other of malicious intent. For example, there was widespread protest against Donald Trump's family separation policy and the subsequent placing of young children in, essentially, cages, all in order to demonstrate a toughness against those who arrive in the United States at unauthorized crossing points. Once the Biden Administration took control of the government on 20 January 2021, it was only a matter of time before critics decried the "Massive Waves" of immigrants arriving the southern border, "pouring into" Texas and other places. Republicans frequently referred to the Biden Administration's immigration policy as nothing more than "open borders."

Americans, for the most part, don't understand that immigration policy is a "federal prerogative" and is set and authorized by Congress and the Executive. Individual states can't make or set immigration policy. Recently, the four states that border Latin America—Arizona, California, New Mexico, and Texas—have begun various attempts at keeping immigrants out of their state. Texas has been the most aggressive (the other three states have Democratic governors): in 2023, the state of Texas set up a floating barrier in the Rio Grande to prevent people from arriving at Eagle Pass. A federal judge ordered the state to remove the barriers, as their placement in the river violates treaty obligations between the United States and Mexico.

In 2022, things were even stranger. On September 14, 2022, 49 people from Venezuela were asked to sign a document and board a charted jetliner—they had arrived in San Antonio, Texas, and had been paroled into the country, meaning they were released into the United States to await a future hearing before an immigration judge. Ron DeSantis, the governor of Florida, put together a scheme whereby these people were picked up in Texas and shipped to Martha's Vineyard, a small island off the coast of Massachusetts known for its liberal traditions and values: Carly Simon lives there; the Obamas and the Clintons vacationed there. The 49 travelers had no idea where they were going: They were told that they would have housing and jobs upon arrival—which was not true.

The good people of the Vineyard embraced the Venezuelans and helped them settle in Massachusetts and nearby. Ironically, these people who were deceptively transported from Texas to Massachusetts are likely eligible for a special type of "U-Visa"—a class of visa designated for folks who have been the victims of crimes in the Unites States and need special protection. This inhumane "dumping" of 49 Venezuelans on a remote, tiny Massachusetts island is part of a relatively new strategy by the governors of Texas and Florida; they claim that their states are especially "burdened" by arriving immigrants, and they want to share this burden with northern Democratic states and cities. New York City and Chicago have been particularly affected. The mayor of New York, reacting to busloads of migrants arriving to his city, claimed—in a fit of exasperation—that immigrants were "destroying" his city. He made these remarks in September 2023.

But it's also true that state economies that encourage immigration and support immigrants are stronger than those where immigrants are neither wanted nor encouraged to live. California versus West Virginia. Texas versus North Dakota. California and Texas are robust, successful, complex economies and societies thanks in large measure to copious numbers of immigrants—documented and otherwise—who are there to work! All people, it must be remembered, pay into local coffers by paying state and local sales taxes; they pay real estate taxes indirectly by paying rents to landlords, and those who have taxpayer ID numbers or the NIT contribute to the US social security system to the tune of billions of dollars every year. So, the facile argument on the far right claiming that undocumented immigrants are nothing but a drain on our economy? Those arguments have been debunked with data and economic analysis.

Some Policy Options

People have recently spoken about "Parole" to the United States from Venezuela, Haiti, Cuba, and Nicaragua: all nations of Latin America with which the United States has limited or troubled relations. As of this writing, there is no functioning government in Haiti. The United States and

Venezuela have limited diplomatic relations, and the same holds true for our relationships with Cuba (dating back to the final days of the Eisenhower administration in 1961) and Nicaragua. All three nations (Cuba, Nicaragua, and Venezuela) have forged an economic and political path that has not been favorably looked upon by the United States. In October 2022, the Biden Administration, in an attempt to control the chaos at the southern border, offered Parole status to 30,000 people per month from the four nations mentioned above. "Parole" would be offered to people who applied through a US government app. They would have to fly to the United States and mention the name of someone in the United States who could serve as a sponsor.

The Biden Administration has been trying to impose a more orderly process of migration, but without a comprehensive overhaul of our outdated immigration laws—the last comprehensive immigration reform was passed during the Reagan Administration in 1987. Presidential decrees, actions, and executive orders fall far short of what's needed for people desperate to live and work in the United States. In September 2023, acknowledging the reality of tens of thousands of Venezuelans in US cities, the Biden Administration offered people who "walked" into the country via the dangerous and much publicized Darién Route the opportunity to stay for at least 18 months and receive work authorization.[4] These are not criminals—they're people who have been vetted at the border, and they've come here to work, earn money, and send money home to loved ones left behind.

TPS

In 2021, Venezuela was designated with temporary protective status; such status is determined by the Executive Branch, via the Secretary of Homeland Security. It is designed to help people who are living in the United States with irregular documentation, offering them a low to no priority status for deportation—assuming they've committed no criminal acts in the United States. TPS has been used to protect people who have fled natural disasters back home and, in many cases, have no home to return to. It's also been used to offer protection to people in the United States who are unwelcome in their homes due to their political or social views; Venezuela, El Salvador, and Haiti have not protected dissidents or those openly hostile to the governments in those places. The logic of TPS? Let people live here as long as possible until the socioeconomic situation improves back home. Recently, in September 2023, TPS for Venezuela was extended for another 18 months.

But then the policy shifted again as the Biden Administration announced that Venezuelans who arrived "illegally" to the United States would be deported back to Caracas via deportation flights. These flights were approved once the Venezuelan government agreed to accept returning (or returned) migrants. Given the skeleton diplomatic relations that currently exist between Caracas and Washington, negotiating these transfers proved time consuming and contentious.

Certainly, the Biden Administration has sought to support Venezuelans who have a legitimate reason to leave that nation: its economy is in shambles, and the leadership is mercurial (at best) and downright dictatorial at worst. In 2024, the president of the nation faced the Venezuelan electorate, and, since we know past is prologue, the international community witnessed a less than robust, transparent contest. It's almost unimaginable to consider the out-migration of 25 percent of a nation's population, but that is what in fact has happened in Venezuela—an oil rich, once-wealthy South American nation that has been driven to despair due to international sanctions, corruption, and uninspired leadership. The people who have been traveling are young—if the press photos are any indication—and it takes a certain degree of stamina, youth, and optimism to travel by foot from Caracas to the US border. Some of those who have made the journey, and their stories, will be the focus of the next section of this chapter.

Not all Venezuelans struggle through the Darién Gap in order to arrive in the United States. Many have adopted different routes—heading west and south toward Colombia, Ecuador, Chile, and Argentina among other places. The migration story of one Venezuelan, the writer María Teresa Canelones, has been documented by the anthropologist J. Bret Crosson. Crosson reminds us of the magnitude of the crisis: "Of over 7 million Venezuelans who have fled … since 2015, about 6 million have settled in other Latin American countries."[5] The harrowing journeys of Ms Canelones, the negative assumptions that followed her, and the variety of humiliating tasks performed along the journey (not all work is "honorable") reflect the struggles of migrants, and the sociocultural conditions that prevent them from thriving, even in "other" Latin American nations. Canelones and Crosson emphasize the resilience, strength, and optimism of the migrants, rather than assigning them to the "suffering slot" as per more traditional anthropological writing and discourse. The "Dark Anthropology" of the past has been reframed, to some extent, to an anthropology of hope. The collaboration between the writer/subject/migrant on the move and the anthropologist on faculty at the second wealthiest university in the United States (University of Texas at Austin) is memorable and remarkable.

Veronica Sánchez is from the Central region of Venezuela and arrived in the United States about two years ago.

> In Venezuela we live under a dictatorship, and the situation is deplorable: We don't have electricity, water, or access to natural gas – the basic

> services. Salaries are miserable – maybe seven dollars per month! Some, with luck, can earn 30 dollars per month.

She continued,

> It's very comfortable here in Texas; I've been able to work here and – I'm from the LGBTI community and I've been able to be who I am here. There's a lot of discrimination against people like me in Venezuela. I've never felt discriminated against, here.[6]

While many nations of Latin America—supposedly conservative, Catholic, and traditional nations—have opened up rights for the LGBTI community (Argentina, Brazil, Chile, Mexico, Colombia immediately come to mind), Venezuela is a different story, and it's not surprising that a member of the LGBTI community would leave there and seek asylum here in the United States. Veronica is one example of how legal discrimination harms a population and leads to out-migration. A statute, for example, in the Venezuelan Code of Miliary Justice which punished homosexual acts by one to three years in prison, was overturned in Caracas—in February 2023. Venezuela falls to the bottom—together with Paraguay, Guyana, and Suriname—with respect to LGBTI rights in South America.

The story of Boris Barroso presents a distinct path to Venezuelans leaving the South American nation to live in the United States. Barroso is a 77-year-old scholar who currently works as a professor at the William J. Perry Center for Hemispheric Studies at the National Defense University in Washington, D.C. We spoke to him by telephone in late October 2023.

Barroso graduated from the Venezuelan Airforce Academy in Maracay in 1968 and visited the United States for the first time shortly thereafter: "I was a devoted New York Yankees fan and wanted to visit Yankee Stadium in New York." Later, he trained in the United States and worked as a flight instructor with the US Navy for three years. He's been living in the United States for 28 years and has been with the Perry Center since it was created in 1997. He wanted to contribute to academic research and scholarship on the hemisphere and completed a master's degree at the Elliot School (George Washington University) and a PhD in Spain. He became a US citizen 14 years ago (in 2010). He applied earlier, but the 2001 terrorist attacks in the United States delayed the process significantly.

At the Perry Center, Prof Barroso has participated in creating the curriculum, teaching students, and conducting research; his doctorate deals with "Cyber security" issues. He left Venezuela because he was interested in expanding his academic and intellectual horizons, something he wasn't able to really achieve in Venezuela in the 1990s. "Venezuela was, in 1995 when I left, a sort of regular, average South American nation with lots of oil reserves, but then things changed in 1999 with the political rise of Mr. Chávez." He continued, "there's a need for structural changes in Venezuela that hopefully will happen in the future—I'm not offended by the political situation there, but I hope structural change occurs before too long."[7]

Today, the media and to some degree academic focus is on the dramatic stories of people literally "walking" to the border separating Latin America and the United States. Barroso's story is different and suggests a long tradition of integration and collaboration between US and Venezuelan institutions that is presently, and sadly, absent. Migration from Venezuela to the United States has occurred for centuries, for a wide variety of reasons, and the immediate and present crisis tends to occlude the stories and migratory processes that predate the present situation.

Isabel Castro is a 23-year-old student who sat with us for an interview in April 2023. She's the only Venezuelan student at the small liberal arts college she attends in the US south. She arrived here in 2016 when the "window" of democratic structures in her native land began to close, and it became a foregone conclusion that "Mr. Maduro would win the presidential elections of 2018"[8] [the OAS declared significant irregularities in those elections].

Isabel's father arrived in the Houston, Texas, area in 2007 to work in the oil industry and was able to bring his family to the United States. Currently, Ms Castro holds the "Green Card" and is applying for US citizenship. She is involved in immigration rights issues at her college (she graduated with degrees in International Studies and Economics). "Americans," says Ms Castro, "need to understand the role their nation has played in pushing people out of their countries of origin." She believes that "TPS should be widely expanded" and states that any and all immigration reform offered by the US government/congress "must contain a strong human rights platform and base."[9]

Edgar Villareal was born in Caracas in 1969 and currently works as head chef in Washington, D.C. He grew up there but spent considerable time moving between Caracas and New York, and later Miami. He established himself as a presence in the Miami food scene during the first decade of this century, "but that scene sort of collapsed with the US economy in '09." At that point, Mr Villareal returned to Caracas with his family and set up a restaurant and also worked in social work; but he returned to the United States for good in 2015. "I saw people in 2015 taking food out of the garbage at my restaurant – that was really terrible to see."[10]

Mr Villareal demurred when asked about the current political crisis in his home nation. "I try to see things in a way that focuses on better days ahead in Venezuela." He illustrated this by discussing his "daily staff meetings" at his restaurant in Caracas:

> Each day at about 11:30, the staff would meet –my staff was young, mostly 20 year olds or 22 year olds and they only knew the excesses of

Chávez and Maduro: I explained to them that there was a long, vibrant tradition in our nation before the current crisis, and tried to help them see that things might improve.

Mr Villareal continued by explaining how much he loves his country: "One of the challenges of living here in the USA is that it's not Venezuela—I miss the smells, the sounds, and the city of Caracas." He acknowledged the many benefits of living here as a resident (Since 2000). "My 19-year-old son is studying on a full scholarship at FIU in Miami and so I'm very grateful—we've very grateful—for that and other opportunities here."

Venezuela, one of the world's richest nations if oil "underground" is taken into consideration, is struggling through international sanctions, repressive, unenlightened government, and a catastrophic out-migration translating to roughly a quarter of the nation's population having fled the South American nation in the past ten years or so. Venezuelans have traveled all over the Americas, including to the United States seeking a better life, and opportunities to work, thrive, and live in dignity. It's a common narrative for all peoples interviewed in this book—the US "migration crisis" will end when sociopolitical and economic conditions in the seven sending nations improve.

Notes

1 See John V. Lombardi, *Venezuela: The Search for Order, the Dream of Progress*. New York: Oxford U. Press, 1982, p. 328.
2 See Michael J. LaRosa and Germán R. Mejía, *An Atlas and Survey of Latin American History*, 2nd ed., Routledge: New York, 2019, p. 179.
3 See Mark T. Gilderhus, David C. LaFevor and Michael J. LaRosa, *The Third Century: U.S. Latin American Relations since 1889*. 2nd ed., Lanham, MD: Rowman and Littlefield Publishers, Inc. 2017, pp. 257–258.
4 See recent work by Julia Turkowitz and Federico Rios, in *The New York Times*, particularly October 24, 2023, "She Heeded Biden's Warning about Immigration: Will She Regret It?".
5 Canelones, M.T. & Crosson, J.B. (2023) Breaking the heart's borders: From "dark anthropology" to dark humor in the telling of migration. *Sociology Lens*, 36(1) p. 123. From Arena, M., Fernandez Corugedo, E., Guajardo, J. and Francisco Yepez, J. (2022) *Venezuela's Migrants Bring Economic Opportunity to Latin America*. IMF (International Monetary Fund) News.
6 Interview with Veronica Sánchez in San Marcos, Texas. Interviewed September 2023 by Tanner M. Neidhardt and sent to authors.
7 Interview with B. Barroso, via telephone, October 23, 2023. Interviewee was located in Washington, D.C.
8 Interview with I. Castro, Memphis TN, April 3, 2023.
9 Interview with I. Castro, Memphis TN, April 3, 2023.
10 Interview with E. Villareal on 1November, 15, 2023, from Washington, D.C.

8

CONCLUSION

One Hundred Years Since Johnson-Reed

As we write up the conclusion to this text, in early 2024, 100 years have elapsed since the first comprehensive immigration reform legislation emerged from the US Congress. The most recent comprehensive reform bill was signed by President Ronald Reagan in 1986—38 years ago.

What a difference 100 years makes! Our first immigration law was drafted in the aftermath of the First World War, the Russian (Bolshevik) Revolution and during the first "Red Scare." It was wholly designed to keep "troublesome" Europeans from our shores and mainly focused on our adversaries from the First World War. People from Germany, the former Austro-Hungarian Empire, and Russia were discriminated against. US animosity toward the Chinese was well established via the "Chinese Exclusion Act" signed into law in 1882 and left on the books until 1943 (the Magnuson Act repealed the Exclusion act).

But Johnson-Reed excluded any mention of the "western hemisphere"—i.e., the Americas. Latin America, the Caribbean, South America, Mexico: None of these places were seen as "problematic" from an immigration or a cultural point of view.

One hundred years later, the US Congress, following the lead of a presidential candidate, refused to act on even moderate immigration reform. In late 2023, Donald Trump, the Republican Candidate for the presidency in 2024, described immigrants who were coming to the United States as "poisoning the blood of our country," a frightening reference to a 20th-century "leader" who is perhaps the most infamous human in modern history.

DOI: 10.4324/9781003357605-9

We have not hidden our perspective in the pages that precede this conclusion. Immigrants are not poisoning our blood, but they are contributing to our communities, helping to grow our economy, taking care of our elderly and working relentlessly to support family and loved ones back in the seven nations about which we write.

How did the political discourse on immigration become so toxic and dangerous? We think at least five internal factors need to be considered: First, the United States, since about 1980 or so, has been deindustrializing with good, once middle-class jobs (protected by labor unions) having been systematically shipped offshore. Deindustrialization helps the owner class and shareholders to cut costs and increase profits—profits they rarely pass on to the middle or lower classes. Changes in technology and advances in shipping have allowed this to occur gradually while dramatically shrinking our "middle class."

Second, both political parties have worked to shrink the middle class. Ronald Reagan's basic distrust of the government led to the theory (or was the result of a theory) that the private sector would always work more efficiently and with greater efficacy than the government. The theory, of course, evaporated once the COVID-19 crisis hit and the private sector of the United States literally collapsed, begging for (and receiving) massive government subsidies.

Third, technological change has forced an immediacy on American life that would have been unimaginable two decades ago. Technology has also eliminated many positions in retail and other sectors of the economy, and when Americans can't find decent positions at decent pay, they tend to lash out at "others" and blame these mysterious others for their own precarious economic position. We could go back to at least 1882, the Chinese Exclusion Act, to explore this phenomenon in greater detail.

The COVID-19 crisis didn't help matters much. It led to a great wave of fear, isolation, and a massive, almost unimaginable death toll in the world (with 1.2 million deaths in the United States, as of this writing), and it led, sadly, to the kind of magical thinking that is nice to see in literary texts, but not so nice to see in congressional debates, journalistic accounts, or political campaigns. The emergence of "Q-anon" seems like it could only happen in a parallel universe when one carefully studies the precepts of the movement. Now there are advocates of this "theory" sitting in the US Congress, most notably the congresswoman from Northwest Georgia, Marjorie Taylor Greene.

Finally, the media needs to provide 24-hour-a-day coverage in order to maintain profitability. The truth of what's being reported matters less than the vividness, the intensity of coverage, or the "excitement" generated by the issue. Images of poor people arriving at the southwest border are not new: What is new is the news coverage which overwhelmingly characterizes these people as a potential problem for the nation; the media rarely, if ever, attempts to understand who these people are, or why they've traveled overland (or crossed the Caribbean Sea) to arrive at the United States.

Our book has attempted to tell that side of the story. We've also tried to connect immigration from the seven nations under study to US policy, over a long period of time. The only way forward on immigration is for Congress to act with determination, in a bipartisan fashion, to help bring some order and coherence to the contemporary situation.

Immigration policy is the purview of the federal government: Individual states can neither make nor enforce immigration policy—it's a federal matter. Despite this long-established understanding, some states, specifically Texas, have taken to enforcing their own brand of immigration policy by setting up razor wire barriers and arresting people who arrive at unauthorized crossing points. SB4 is the name of this legislation—and currently it's being tossed back-and-forth by the courts. The Governor of Texas, Greg Abbot, is using a get-tough-on-immigrants approach to launch a probable, future presidential campaign. Most Americans, we believe, will be unimpressed to learn that the governor authorized the placing of concertina wire in the river, defying the United States and in violations of established treaties between the United States and Mexico. Harming children by cutting them with Razor Wire is the exact opposite of what the United States stands for.

Despite the razor wire, the mean-spirited governor, and the laws, the people keep coming here. As we've tried to explain in the previous pages, there is a reason for this: the United States remains—despite its many flaws—the one and final hope for many people fleeing poverty, violence, misery, and hopelessness. The stories we've presented above attest to some of this misery. Haiti, as we write this concluding chapter, has essentially become a failed state, given that criminal gangs have pushed the acting president out of office as a search begins for legitimate political candidates. Unfortunately, some of the people directing and animating the gangs of Port-au-Prince hope to present as presidential candidates. The United States has been reluctant to involve itself in this situation, and the United Nations' last foray into Haiti ended badly—with a cholera epidemic in Haiti blamed on Nepalese troops sent by the UN.

Cubans and Venezuelans continue to arrive in the United States. Their economies have been undermined by a US embargo in the first case (an embargo that has been on the books since early 1962) and deep sanctions imposed by the Trump Administration (and others) in the second. These economic policies have hurt the two economies and have left little space for ordinary people to eke out a living. Hence, the people travel north. In the case of Venezuela, about 20 percent of the population has left the nation—or 7.5 million people—in recent years. Many have settled in neighboring Colombia, which has absorbed perhaps 1.8 million Venezuelans, but many hope to make it to the United States, and some are willing to literally "walk" from Venezuela to the southern border, through Colombia, through a dense jungle separating Colombia and Panama, transversing Central American and Mexico. A truly daunting journey.

Colombia is another nation under study in this text. The nation is governed by a democratically elected, progressive president, Mr Gustavo Petro. He has not been able to completely control the nation of some 50 million people, and the "Bacrím" (Criminal Gangs), a legacy of the half-century-long insurgencies against the Colombian state, hold outsized power and persuasion in many sectors of the nation—particularly on the north coast. Though the largest and most powerful insurgency (the FARC) laid down their weapons in widely celebrated 2016 peace accords, many people see "same old situation, different actors" with the relatively newly minted Criminal networks.

The Central American nations under study here—Honduras and Guatemala—have struggled in recent years: Political corruption in both cases has been systemic, and natural catastrophes have affected both nations, particularly Honduras which was devastated some 25 years ago by Hurricane Mitch. In Guatemala, the United States' political and military intervention in 1954 dramatically changed the nation's history, keeping the somewhat medieval social hierarchy largely intact. The Civil War there, which lasted from 1960 to 1996, was characterized by deep racial hatred and genocide against indigenous peoples. Guatemala has never quite recovered from the excesses of the 20th century, though Peace Accords were signed in 1996.

In Mexico, the nation that shares a nearly 1,900-mile border with the United States and a long history of antagonism and intervention, the "border" separates the North American first world (the United States and Canada) from the rest of the world. People from every corner of the world attempt to cross, by land, into the United States via Mexico at this vast, mostly unregulated and unenforced border. Mexicans who labor in Mexico for an $8 dollar-a-day minimum wage want and expect more from life. They see a desert/border separating them from a distinct reality in the north. Many choose to cross without proper documentation at an unregulated (and dangerous) desert crossing. Many die trying to do so, and others still remember the difficult journey, the lack of water, and the hunger faced during the crossing—as reported by Adam Reyes, two decades after his crossing from Mexico to the United States.

Americans justifiably ask, "why can't they just get in line?" and the answer is simple. There is no line. It's nearly impossible for a poor (i.e., economically disadvantaged) Mexican without special skills to seek and receive an official visa from the US embassy or a consulate in Mexico. For this reason, we have called for a general, comprehensive immigration reform—which can only come from the US Congress, to harmonize our economic reality (the United States desperately needs workers in most sectors of the economy) with our own declining demographic reality. This should be an easy, bipartisan agenda item, but it's become in recent years a pitched battle between the parties. The result has been no serious immigration reform in decades and to revisit the most recent, comprehensive reform signing ceremony, one would have to travel back to the Reagan Administration!

If we're lucky, we all live in Cities of Immigrants—to borrow a phrase made popular by singer/songwriter Steve Earle in 2007. He continues, "In the sacred promise a statue made / Livin' in a city of immigrants." That sacred promise is still sacred, but the promise is certainly under attack by people who fail to understand the promise, the hope offered by the United States. People, recently, have run out of imagination and seem to lack the perspective that allows them to see all our histories/stories as interconnected. We think this anti-immigrant resurgence is temporary; we believe this because we've studied the historic record, and anti-immigrant waves are always followed by something different, more refreshing and enlightening.

America survives only by traveling together with the world community—a world we don't necessarily lead any longer, but one to which we're intimately, historically, and existentially connected.

APPENDIX A

Legal

This history of immigration policy in the United States is a pendulum swinging back-and-forth between liberalized policy—allowing for the admission of more immigrants or particular groups—and anti-immigrant sentiment—advocating closed borders or tight restrictions on who can enter the United States. For the past 100 years, this pendulum has affected general immigration policy but also how we look at immigration for countries of the Western Hemisphere and particularly the seven countries examined in this book.

In 1924, Congress enacted the *Johnson-Reed Act*, which came on the heels of a number of anti-immigrant laws that specifically targeted and restricted immigration from Asian and Eastern/Southern European countries. The *Johnson-Reed Act* ratcheted down a quota system that limited immigration to the United States to 2 percent of the number of foreign-born individuals of each nationality who resided in the United States based on the 1890 census. This quota system reduced overall immigration but also favored countries such as the United Kingdom and Germany, while disfavoring countries like Italy and China. While it did not apply to the countries of the Western Hemisphere, the *Johnson-Reed Act* largely exemplifies the sentiment toward immigrants at that time. Further, as the economy tightened as a result of the Great Depression, hundreds of thousands of Mexicans and Mexican Americans were deported or coerced into leaving for Mexico.

As a result of the Second World War, public opinion on immigration shifted for practical and moral reasons. For example, in 1942, the United

States and Mexico implemented the *Bracero Program*, which allowed thousands of Mexican workers to come to the United States to work on short-term contracts to make up for the thousands of American workers fighting in the war. Congress also began to adopt revisions to immigration law that sought to remedy the restrictions that had led to the United States turning back thousands of Jews and other persecuted groups before and during the Second World War.

For example, President John F. Kennedy signed into law the *Migration and Refugee Assistance Act of 1962*, which empowered the government to meet the needs of refugees and displaced persons. Congress specifically designed this law to assist Cubans fleeing Castro's communist regime in the days after the Cuban Revolution.

In 1965, Lyndon Johnson signed the *Immigration and Nationality Act of 1965 (INA)*, which may be the most significant civil rights law ever passed in how it remade the complexion of America. The *INA* abolished discriminatory quotas based on nationality and in its place created a system that gave preference to family reunification as well as certain professions and skills, though it did place a cap of 120,000 on the total number of immigrants from the Western Hemisphere. Congress later amended that cap, allowing a ceiling of 20,000 from each country in the Western Hemisphere to immigrate each year. Congress amended the *INA* again in 1978 to set a ceiling of 290,000 immigrants per year, worldwide, to the United States.

In 1980 in the wake of the Vietnam War, Congress passed the *Refugee Act of 1980*, which raised the ceiling of refugees per year from 17,400 to 50,000. The act also recognized

> the historic policy of the United States to respond to the urgent needs of persons subject to persecution in their homelands, including, … [providing] humanitarian assistance for their care and maintenance in asylum areas, efforts to promote opportunities for resettlement or voluntary repatriation, … admission to this country of refugees of special humanitarian concern to the United States, and transitional assistance to refugees in the United States.[1]

In 1986, Ronald Reagan signed the *Immigration Reform and Control Act (IRCA)*, which sought to address the issue of unauthorized immigration by implementing an employment verification program and penalizing employers who knowingly employed undocumented workers. *IRCA* also created a pathway to citizenship for roughly three million, mostly Latino, individuals.

Four years later, in 1990, Congress passed the *Immigration Act of 1990*, which among other reforms created *Temporary Protected Status (TPS)* in which the attorney general (now secretary of Homeland Security) could grant nationals from a foreign country temporary protected status and work authorization if they were unable to safely return to their home countries due to armed conflict, natural disaster, or other extraordinary conditions.[2]

By the mid-1990s, *IRCA* proved itself to be ineffective in reducing the overall level of undocumented immigration and a growing anti-immigrant sentiment developed. President Bill Clinton, in a prime example of his famed triangulation, signed the *Illegal Immigration Reform and Immigrant Responsibility Act of 1996 (IIRAIRA)*, which bolstered immigration laws by making it a crime for an employer to hire an undocumented immigrant and increased penalties on undocumented immigrants who committed crimes while in the United States.

Despite this shifting sentiment, the United States retained its commitment to assisting refugees and asylum seekers by passing the *Nicaraguan Adjustment and Central American Relief Act (NACARA)* in 1997 and the *Haitian Refugee Immigration Fairness Act (1998)*, which created a pathway to permanent residency for Nicaraguans, Cubans, Salvadorans, Guatemalans, and Haitians as well as those from the former Soviet bloc countries who had come to the United States seeking asylum.

By the late 1990s and early 2000s, it was clear to most that the American immigration system was broken. Senators John McCain (R-AZ) and Ted Kennedy (D-MA) pushed for comprehensive immigration reform known as "*CIR*" or the "*McCain-Kennedy Bill.*" This bill created major reforms of the immigration systems including increased border security as well as immigration relief for DREAMers or individuals who as children entered the United States without inspection or overstayed visas. Ultimately, the momentum behind *CIR* stagnated under an increasingly nativist/protectionist shift in society. As a result, the *Secure Fence Act of 2006* passed, authorizing money and resources to build a portion of a wall along the southern border.

In 2012, President Obama took executive action to address the precarious situation of the DREAMers and created *Deferred Action for Childhood Arrivals (DACA)*, which granted deferred action and work authorization for individuals who entered before the age of 16 and had been continuously present in the United States for the five years before the signing of the executive action. A further effort to expand deferred action to the parents of DREAMers, called *DAPA*, was struck down by the courts. *DACA* also sits in a precarious situation—under attack in the courts as well as threatened by a potential change in presidential administrations.

In 2024, a bipartisan group of senators put together an immigration reform that for a brief moment raised the hope of change. Former President Donald Trump, however, torpedoed any chance of passage in an effort to keep this campaign issue alive to benefit his political aspirations. Future reform seems unlikely as congressional leaders have grown more concerned with using the issue for political points instead of trying to actually fix the system.

Notes

1 8 U.S.C. § 1521, note (congressional declaration of policies and objectives).
2 12 U.S.C. § 1254a(b)(1)(A)-(C).

APPENDIX B

Films and Documentaries

A Day Without a Mexican. (2004). Directed by Sergio Arau. USA.
All the Pretty Horses. (2000). Directed by Billy Bob Thornton. USA.
El Norte. (1983). Directed by Gregory Nava. USA.
Icebox. (2018). Directed by Danial Sawka. USA.
La Nava de los Sueños. (1996). Directed by Ciro Durán. Colombia.
Maria Full of Grace. (2004). Directed by Joshua Marston. USA/Colombia.
Mi Familia. (1995). Directed by Gregory Nava. USA.
Sin Nombre. (2009). Directed by Cary Joji Fukunaga. USA.
The Three Burials of Melquiades Estrada. (2005). Directed by Tommy Lee Jones. USA.
Under the Same Moon. (2007). Directed by Patricia Riggen. USA.
Visa USA. (1986). Directed by Lisandro Duque Naranjo. Colombia.
Who is Dayani Cristal? (2013). Documentary. Directed by Marc Silver. USA.

APPENDIX C

Seven Other Sources to Help Think About Immigration

1. **The Art of Álvaro Enciso.** Álvaro Enciso is a migrant from Colombia who has lived most of his life in the United States. For the past ten years or so, the Tucson-based artist has been making weekly forays into the Sonoran Desert to mark the spot where migrants have died while traveling to the United States. Most die from dehydration. Since 1981, it is estimated that 3,800 people have died, though that number is most likely much higher. Mr. Enciso leaves a hand-made cross behind at the site and has named his project "Donde Los Sueños Mueran"—where dreams die.
2. **The Immigration *retablos* of Nicario Jiménez Q.** Artist Nicario Jiménez, since 1990, has been creating art-work based on the migrant experience from South America to the United States. A Peruvian immigrant who has lived the majority of his life in the United States (presently based in Naples, Florida), Nicario's first immigration piece dates from 1990 and is called "Border Patrol"—and is now part of a private collection. His most recent work dealing with immigration is titled "La Bestia" [the Beast], and depicts the epic struggles/travel of people who ride atop the trains that move through Mexico to the border with the United States.
3. **National Immigration Project.** This association of lawyers has been working for about 50 years to defend immigrant rights in the United States and has been seeking a more standardized, progressive policy to support immigrants. The attorneys associated with this group conduct advocacy work; they teach and work to educate the public on the extremely complex immigration system currently "deployed" in the United States. The complexity is deliberate, to some degree, as each state is allowed to make laws restricting immigration, but immigration policy,

enforcement, and more standardized laws are the purview of the federal government.

4. **Doctors for Immigrants** is an organization based out of California, founded by Dr. Ataf Saaida. Their slogan "no one should be afraid to seek medical care" nicely sums up a contemporary conundrum in the United States. People with irregular immigration status and/or no medical insurance delay medical treatment, which sometimes results in permanent injury or death. Physicians in the United States are primarily concerned with patient care—as per the Hippocratic Oath—but in one instance from 1994, California passed a ballot initiative that forced physicians to ask about immigration status before treating patients. Physicians mostly ignored this mandate, and the law, by 1999, was declared unconstitutional by the California Supreme Court.
5. **Pew Research Center.** The "Pew" is a Washington, D.C.-based "fact tank" organization that provides data and research on a wide variety of topics. The organization is nonpartisan but lilts a little to the progressive left. Their immigration and immigrant research is often quoted in the mainstream media, and their facts, figures, and findings are seen as sober, accurate, and truthful. Michael Dimock is the current president of Pew, a political scientist by training and profession. The data and reports from Pew are presented in an easy-to-absorb format, absent of technical jargon and political drama.
6. **Photographers.** Since the introduction of photography in the 19th century, the art form has captivated the human imagination, brought people together, and informed the public about monumental events. Matthew Brady's work from the Civil War comes to mind as does Jacob Riis's depictions of Italian and Jewish immigrants in New York's Lower East Side, in the early 20th century. Dorothea Lange captured the poverty, dignity, and humanity of migrants in the Southwestern United States in the 1930s. More recently, Richard Misrach, Alex Webb, and Guillermo Arias have produced impressive work depicting the immigrant experience.
7. **Welcoming America.** Fifteen years ago, in 2009, David Lubell established "Welcoming America" and "Welcoming International" after founding TIRRC—the Tennessee Immigration and Refugee Rights Coalition. TIRRC was a successful advocacy organization with the goal of educating people and communities on the net-added value of immigrants. TIRRC and Welcoming America promoted immigrants and immigration as significant contributors to their communities, especially in the deindustrializing South where immigrants were unfairly blamed for crime, low wages, and general mayhem. In fact, Welcoming America has determined that immigrants have been rebuilding communities, boosting property values, and founding local businesses while contributing to the cultural fabric of our society.

BIBLIOGRAPHY

Colombia

Abel, Christopher. "External Philanthrophy and Domestic Change in Colombian Healthcare: The Role of the Rockefeller Foundation, ca. 1920 – 50." *Hispanic American Historical Review* 75 (1995).

Abad, Faciolince Héctor. *The Farm*. New York: Archipelago Books. 2018.

Braun, Herbert. *Our Guerrilla, Our Sidewalks*. 2nd Ed. Landham: Roman & Littlefield Publishers. 2003.

Farnsworth-Alvear, Ann; Marco Palacios, and Ana María Gómez López, eds. *The Colombia Reader*. Durham: Duke University Press. 2016.

LaRosa, Michael J., and Germán Mejía Pavony. *Colombia: A Concise Contemporary History*. 3rd Ed. Landham: Rowman and Littlefield Publishers, Inc., 2023.

Paternostro, Silvana. *My Colombian War*. New York: Henry Holt and Company. 2013.

Randall, Stephen. *Colombia and the United States: Hegemony and Interdependence*. Athens: University of Georgia Press. 1992.

Restrepo, Laura. *Leopard in the Sun*. New York: Crown Publishing Group. 1999.

Vásquez, Juan Gabriel. *The Sound of Things Falling*. New York: Riverhead Books. 2013.

Waters, Mary C.; Reed Veda; and Helen B. Marrow, eds. *The New Americans: A Guide to Immigration Since 1965*. Cambridge: Harvard University Press. 2007.

Cuba

Arenas, Reinaldo. *Before Night Falls*. New York: Penguin. 1993.

Behar, Ruth. *Traveling Heavy: A Memoir In Between Journeys*. Durham: Duke University Press. 2013.

Chomsky, Aviva; Barry Carr, Alfredo Prieto and Pamela Maria Smorkaloff, eds. *The Cuba Reader*. Durham: Duke University Press. 2019.
Eire, Carlos. *Waiting for Snow in Havana*. Washington: The Free Press. 2004.
Ferrer, Ada. *Cuba: An American History*. New York: Scribner. 2021.
García, Cristina. *Dreaming in Cuban*. New York: Alfred A. Knopf. 1992.
Levine, Robert M. *Tropical Diaspora*. Gainesville: University of Florida Press. 1993.
Padilla, Heberto. *Self-Portrait of the Other*. New York: Farrar, Straus and Giroux. 1990.
Pérez Firmat, Gustavo. *Next Year in Cuba*. Houston: Arte Público Press. 2006.
Pérez, Louis A., Jr. *On Becoming Cuban*. Chapel Hill: University of North Carolina Press. 2008.

Guatemala

Asturias, Miguel. *Señor Presidente*. New York: Macmillan. 1963.
Capeland, Nicolas. *The Democracy Development Machine: Neoliberalism, Radical Pessimism, and Authoritarian Populism in Mayan Guatemala*. Ithaca: Cornell. 2019.
Immerman, Richard. *The CIA in Guatemala*. Austin: University of Texas Press. 1982.
Goldman, Francisco. *The Art of Political Murder*. New York: Grove Press. 2008.
Grandin, Greg; Deborah T. Levenson and Elizabeth Oglesby, eds. *The Guatemalan Reader*. Durham: Duke University Press. 2011.
Handy, Jim. *Gift of the Devil*. Boston: South End Press. 1984.
Menchú Tum, Rigoberta. *I Rigoberta Menchú*. 2nd Ed. New York: Verso. 2010.
Perera, Victor. *Unfinished Conquest*. Los Angeles: University of California Press. 1993.
Schlesinger, Stephen and Stephen Kinzer. *Bitter Fruit*. New York: Anchor. 1983.
Weld, Kirsten. *Paper Cadavers: The Archives of Dictatorship in Guatemala*. Durham: Duke University Press. 2014.

Haiti

Byrd, Brandon R. *The Black Republic: African-Americans and the Fate of Haiti*. Philadelphia: University of Pennsylvania Press. 2019.
Casimir, Jean. *The Haitians: A Decolonial History*. Translated by Laurent Dubois. Chapel Hill: University of North Carolina Press. 2020.
Coupeau, Steeve. *The History of Haiti*. Westport CT: Greenwood Press. 2007.
Calargé, Carla; Rapael Dalleo, Luis Duno-Gottbert and Clevis Headley, eds. *Haiti and the Americas*. Jackson: U. Mississippi Press. 2013.
Danticat, Edwidge. *Brother, I'm Dying*. New York: Alfred A. Knopf. 2007.
Dubois, Laurent. *Haiti: The Aftershocks of History*. London: Picador. 2013.
Fournier, Arthur. *The Zombie Curse*. Washington: Joseph Henry Press. 2006.
Fournier, Arthur. *Hope Makes Us Live! Hope Makes Us Die!* London: Olympia Publishers. 2023.
Girard, Philippe. *Haiti: The Tumultuous History from Pearl of the Caribbean to Broken Nation*. New York: Palgrave Macmillan. 2010.

Girard, Philippe. *Clinton in Haiti: The 1994 U.S. Intervention in Haiti*. New York: Palgrave Macmillan. 2004.

Trouillot, Michel-Rolph. *Silencing the Past: Power and the Production of History*. Boston: Beacon Press. 1995.

Honduras

Blitzer, Jonathan. *Everyone Who Is Gone Is Here: The United States, Central America, and the Making of a Crisis*. New York: Penguin. 2024.

Chomsky, Aviva. *Central America's Forgotten History: Revolution, Violence, and the Roots of Migration*. Boston: Beacon Press. 2021.

Cohen, Rich. *The Fish That Ate the Whale: The Life and Times of American's Banana King*. New York: Farrar, Straus and Giroux. 2012.

Foster, Lynn V. *A Brief History of Central America*. New York: Checkmark Books. 2007.

Frank, Dana. *The Long Honduran Night: Resistance, Terror, and the United States in the Aftermath of the Coup*. Chicago: Haymarket Books. 2018.

LaFeber, Walter. *Inevitable Revolutions: The United States in Central America*. New York: W. W. Norton and Company. 1983.

Murren, James. *Whispers of Honduras: A Peace Corps Experience*. Published by author. 2015.

Sanders, Keyla. *Mojeda: Memoir of a Honduran Immigrant*. Jefferson: McFarland and Company. 2023.

"'There Are No Investigations Here' – Impunity for Killings and Other Abuses in Bajo Aguán, Honduras." *Human Rights Watch*, Feb. 12, 2014, https://www.hrw.org/report/2014/02/12/there-are-no-investigations-here/impunity-killings-and-other-abuses-bajo-aguan

Woodward, Ralph Lee. *Central America: A Nation Divided*. London: Oxford University Press. 1999.

Mexico

Beezley, William H. *Judas at the Jockey Club*. Lincoln: University of Nebraska Press. 1987.

Cohen, Deborah. *Braceros: Migrant Citizens and Transnational Subjects in the Postwar United States and Mexica*. Chapel Hill: University of North Carolina Press. 2011.

Delpar, Helen. *The Enormous Vogue of Things Mexican*. Tuscaloosa: University of Alabama Press. 1995.

Fuentes, Carlos. *The Crystal Frontier*. New York: HarperVia. 1998.

Henderson, Timothy. *Beyond Borders: A History of Mexican Migration to the United States*. Hoboken: Wiley-Blackwell. 2011.

Martínez, Oscar J., ed. *U.S.-Mexico Borderlands: Historical and Contemporary Perspectives*. Landham: Jaguar Books. 1996.

Mendoza, Christina. *Women, Migration, and Domestic Work on the Texas-Mexico Border*. El Paso: LFB Scholarly Publishing LLC. 2011.

Navarro, Sonia. *Enrique's Journey*. New York: Random House. 2006.

Ramos, Jorge. *Dying to Cross*. New York: HarperCollins Publishers. 2006.

Venezuela

Carroll, Rory. *Comandante: Hugo Chávez's Venezuela*. New York: Penguin. 2014.
Coronil, Fernando. *The Magical State: Nature, Money, and Modernity in Venezuela*. Chicago: University of Chicago Press. 1997.
Corrales, Javier and Michael Penfold. *Dragon in the Tropics: The Legacy of Hugo Chávez*. Washington: Brookings Institution Press. 2015.
Ewell, Judith. *Venezuela and the United States*. Athens: University of Georgia Press. 1996.
Gilderhus, Mark T., David C. LaFevor and Michael J. LaRosa. *The Third Century*. Landham: Rowman and Littlefield. 2017.
LaRosa, Michael J., and Germán R. Mejía. *An Atlas and Survey of Latin American History*. 2nd Ed. New York: Routledge. 2018.
Lombardi, John V. *Venezuela: The Search for Order, the Dream of Progress*. London: Oxford University Press. 1982.
Neuman, William. *Things Are Never So Bad That They Can't Get Worse: Inside the Collapse of Venezuela*. New York: St. Martin's Press. 2022.
Tarver, H. Michael and Julia C. Frederick. *The History of Venezuela*. New York: Palgrave, 2006.
Tinker Salas, Miguel. *The Enduring Legacy: Oil, Culture, and Society in Venezuela*. Durham: Duke University Press. 2009.

General Bibliography of Literary and Other Sources

Alire Sáenz, Benjamin. *Everything Begins and Ends at the Kentucky Club*. El Paso: Cinco Puntos Press. 2012.
Anzaldúa, Gloria. *Borderlands / La Frontera: The New Mestiza*. San Francisco: Aunt Lute Books. 1987.
Bender, Steven W. *Run for the Border*. New York: New York University Press. 2012.
Cásares, Oscar. *Brownsville*. Boston: Little, Brown and Company. 2003.
Chacón, Justic Akers and Mike Davis. *No One is Illegal*. Chicago: Haymarket Books. 2006.
Cummins, Jeanine. *American Dirt*. New York: Flatiron Books. 2020.
Damian, Carol; Michael J. LaRosa, and Steve Stein. *Immigration in the Visual Art of Nicario Jiménez Quispe*. Landham: Rowman and Littlefield. 2019.
González, Juan. *Harvest of Empire: A History of Latinos in America*. New York: Penguin. 2001.
LaRosa, Michael J. and Frank O. Mora, eds. *Neighborly Adversaries*. 3rd Ed. Landham: Rowman and Littlefield. 2015.
Luiselli, Valeria. *Lost Children Archive*. New York: Alfred A. Knopf. 2019.
Luiselli, Valeria. *Tell Me How It Ends*. Minneapolis: Coffee House Press. 2017.
McCarthy, Cormac. *All the Pretty Horses*. New York: Alfred A. Knopf. 1992.
Medina Mora, Nicolás. *America del Norte*. New York: Soho Press. 2024.
Migration Policy Institute. *Major U.S. Immigration Laws, 1790 – Present*. 2013.

Ngai, Mae M. *Impossible Subjects: Illegal Aliens and the Making of Modern America*. Princeton: Princeton University Press. 2004.

Quinones, Sam. *Antonio's Gun and Delfino's Dream: True Tales of Mexican Migration*. Albuquerque: University of New Mexico Press. 2008.

Román, Edilberto and Michael A. Olivas *Those Damned Immigrants: America's Hysteria over Undocumented Immigration*. New York: New York University Press. 2013.

Urrea, Luis Alberto. *The House of Broken Angels*. Boston: Little, Brown and Company. 2018.

INDEX

Pages in *italics* refer to figures, pages in **bold** refer to tables, and pages followed by "n" refer to notes.

Made in United States
Cleveland, OH
27 May 2025

17282297R00090